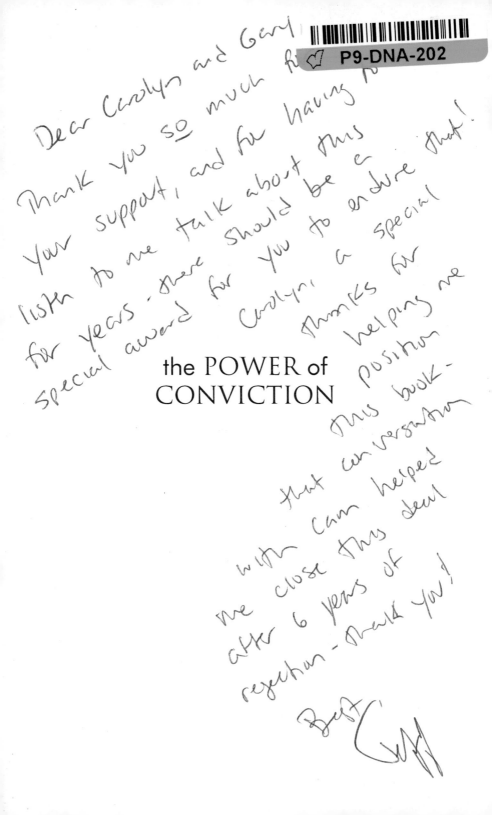

Dear Carolyn and Gary

Thank you so much for
your support, and for having to
listen to me talk about this
for years. There should be a
special award for you to endure that!

Carolyn, a special
thanks for
helping me
position
this book -
that conversation
with Cam helped
me close this deal
after 6 years of
rejection - thank you!

Best,

the POWER of
CONVICTION

the
POWER
C⊕NVICTION

My Wrongful Conviction, 18 Years in Prison
and the Freedom Earned Through
FORGIVENESS and FAITH

JAMES C. TILLMAN
with Jeff Kimball

New York

the POWER of CONVICTION
My Wrongful Conviction, 18 Years in Prison and the
Freedom Earned Through FORGIVENESS and FAITH

© 2015 JAMES C. TILLMAN.

Published in New York, New York, by Morgan James Publishing. Morgan James and The Entrepreneurial Publisher are trademarks of Morgan James, LLC. www.MorganJamesPublishing.com

The Morgan James Speakers Group can bring authors to your live event. For more information or to book an event visit The Morgan James Speakers Group at www.TheMorganJamesSpeakersGroup.com.

bitlit

A **free** eBook edition is available
with the purchase of this print book.

CLEARLY PRINT YOUR NAME ABOVE IN UPPER CASE

Instructions to claim your free eBook edition:
1. Download the BitLit app for Android or iOS
2. Write your name in **UPPER CASE** on the line
3. Use the BitLit app to submit a photo
4. Download your eBook to any device

ISBN 978-1-63047-390-7 paperback
ISBN 978-1-63047-391-4 eBook
ISBN 978-1-63047-392-1 hardcover
Library of Congress Control Number:
2014947604

Cover Design by:
Rachel Lopez
www.r2cdesign.com

Interior Design by:
Bonnie Bushman
bonnie@caboodlegraphics.com

In an effort to support local communities, raise awareness and funds, Morgan James Publishing donates a percentage of all book sales for the life of each book to Habitat for Humanity Peninsula and Greater Williamsburg.

Get involved today, visit
www.MorganJamesBuilds.com

Habitat
for Humanity®
Peninsula and
Greater Williamsburg
Building Partner

Dedicated in loving memory to my brother, Dennis, and my mother-in-law, Ruby Milton; To my mother, Catherine Martin, and in loving memory of June, Amy and Susan Kimball.

TABLE OF CONTENTS

ACKNOWLEDGEMENTS

We could easily fill this book with a list of people who have impacted our lives and specifically James' case. You know from meeting us or being our friend how grateful we are for your love and support. A very special thanks to our mothers, Catherine Martin and June Kimball, and our wives, Bridget and Patty, for their encouragement, unwavering support and belief in us, and this book.

We give glory and thanks to God in all we do.

We know that any person we seek to acknowledge is themselves supported by a network of caregivers, from spouses to family, co-workers and friends. So we recognize that there are so many people we should thank who had an impact on this book and its subject matter; please know we are grateful.

James wishes to thank: my wife, Bridget, for all her love and support, and for being my partner, friend, soul mate and inspiration. I want to thank all of my friends and family, including my brother Willie.

There will always be a very special place in my heart for the Connecticut Innocence Project, including its founder, former Chief Public Defender Gerry Smyth, the Hon. Karen Goodrow and Brian Carlow. Barry Scheck of the national Innocence Project has been extremely supportive as well. McCarter & English provided enormous support to the Connecticut Innocence Project, for which I am grateful. Their work could have stopped there, but a number of people have been very helpful to me since my release, showing me why the firm is held in such high regard, including Tim Fisher (who is now Dean of the UConn Law School), Jane Warren and Tiffany Stevens. Bruce Douglas, Ph.D., Executive Director of the Capital Region Education Council (CREC) and his daughter, changed my life forever when they reached out to me to help me find a job after my release. Sonya and Marc Kunkel have been there to support me professionally and personally, and they will always have my gratitude. John Motley, Principal of Motley Consulting and a former senior executive at Travelers, has been my absolute rock. More than a friend, he's had my back, and given what I've been through, it's hard to offer a higher compliment. Mark Hightower, one of my best friends, has been very supportive, especially when I was released from prison. As a community advocate, he helped teach me how I could help others. Rev. Dr. David L. Massey, Rep. Doug McCrory and everyone at Hopewell Baptist Church have been a model of God's light and love, offering me kindness, support and a place I could call home. Sen. Ken Green took a leading role in defending me and my interests in the Legislature. He and the entire State Legislature should be commended for the way they acted on my behalf. A very special thanks to former Gov. Jodi Rell for the respect, dignity and honor she brought to this process. Katie Heffernan, LCSW, Chief Social Worker, Public Defender Division, was one of the few people to touch my soul in the heart of darkness in prison, and she also helped give me strength as I found my freedom. Although I know he doesn't want the recognition, I have to thank Dr. Grayson, whose counseling helped ease my transition from prison life. As much as I want to forget prison life, I do want to thank the librarians and the staff at Cheshire Correctional Center who treated me with dignity and humanity. Doug Joseph, CPA, MST and the late Larry Davis of Blum Shapiro have been instrumental in handling my taxes and financial issues, along with Ed Wahlberg from Merrill Lynch – they're like my financial dream team, and I would be lost without them. Deputy Fire Chief Terry Waller continues to be a solid and reliable friend. President Mark Scheinberg and everyone at Goodwin College have inspired me to fulfill my dream of earning a college education. Finally, thanks to Jeff Kimball for his talents, wisdom and loving spirit – I couldn't ask for a better writer or a better person to call my friend.

Jeff wishes to thank: my sweet angels Lexi & Elyse; my wife Patty, stepchildren Reilly, Sam, Caroline and Sophie; Jane, Steve, John, Jill, Sue, Jim, Bruce, Terry, Nancy, Renee and the entire Kimball-Kunkel-Lewis family for their love and support. A special thanks to Sonya Kunkel for the introduction to James, and for being a driving force behind this book. Thanks to Jane Warren and Rakan Nimr for reading endless drafts, Lane Bailey for enduring my work on endless drafts and Michael Dunne, Christa Carey Dunn, Carolyn Cohen and Jeff Zucker for their support during the editorial process. Thanks to everyone in the Greens Farms Academy community, whose comfortable embrace I left to begin work on this book. Thanks also to Senator Rockefeller and all my colleagues in Washington and West Virginia for first teaching me about the Power of Conviction. As first time authors with no agents or brand recognition, we spent years trying to get publishers to look at this book. We want to thank the entire Morgan James family for taking a chance on us and recognizing what others didn't: that James and I have a story worth telling, and that no matter how many walls we hit, we weren't giving up. That's why I want to acknowledge my parents, who taught me how to persevere, and forged in me an iron will in my advocacy for others. I also want to acknowledge Amy Lynn Sutherland Kimball, whose spirit guided me throughout a process that started on the first anniversary of her death, and whose courageous battle against cancer inspired me to keep fighting, and to never give up. Thanks most of all to James, for giving me the chance to listen and learn from him over the last six years – the way we worked on this book speaks to the enduring friendship we have, for which I am grateful.

O God, hasten to deliver me; O LORD, hasten to my help!
Let those be ashamed and humiliated who seek my life;
Let those be turned back and dishonored who delight in
*   my hurt.*
Let those be turned back because of their shame who say,
*   "Aha, aha!"*
Let all who seek You rejoice and be glad in You;
And let those who love Your salvation say continually, "Let
*   God be magnified."*
But I am afflicted and needy; Hasten to me, O God!
You are my help and my deliverer; O LORD, do not delay.
                            —Psalm 70

Chapter 1

THE ROOTS OF CONVICTION

My earliest memories come from living in Thomasville, Georgia, a dot of a small town in the country, not far from Tallahassee. Thomasville is located in the heart of what you might call the "deep South." A slice of heaven, it was as far away in every respect from the prison in Connecticut that I would eventually call my home for over 18 years. I was living with my Grandparents, because my Mom was looking for a job back home. Ma also wanted to keep us away from my stepfather for a while, because he was abusive at times. I don't remember much about Georgia–I was very young–but I do very clearly remember how I felt: I felt loved; I felt safe; and I felt comfortable. My Grandparent's house was more than a place to live, it was a home. They had a screened in back porch and a yard. We'd eat grits out on the back porch, and steak, and chicken, and biscuits…and so much more! Man, it was awesome. Food so good you could smell it a block away. My Grandmother would make us do chores, and my Grandfather worked very hard cutting wood and selling it. My Grandparents were good people, and to this day I still think of them a lot. We weren't there long—my Mom eventually sent for us, and when we left Thomasville, it kind of felt like I was being sent to the moon, because our new home in Connecticut couldn't have been more different.

Connecticut is known for its wealth, privilege and charm, with its picturesque early-American villages, luxurious estates and beautiful seaside communities. At the center of it all stands Hartford, one of America's first cities, with the Capitol's radiant gold dome anchoring the skyline. I came of age in Hartford in the 1970s, literally and figuratively in the shadows of the capitol, when it was anything but the vibrant and welcoming city it is today. A time many remember for big hair, tight pants, crazy outfits and disco, I remember living in an empty, desolate city, trash littering the streets, the water polluted so badly it was hard to drink and the sound of desperation that seemed to follow you around every corner. Hartford's economy was in ruins. Poverty and crime rates were on their way to historic highs as people fled to the suburbs, taking the life out of the city, along with most of its jobs. The city was in many ways a lifeless gray concrete façade that hid the lives of people most didn't think about. I was one of those people. This was the Connecticut that I called home. Somewhere in this crumbling city, the values that would later define my life began to take shape: to live a life of conviction: to believe in myself, especially when no one else did; to live in service to God, or something greater than me, even when situations were so dire it seemed that God wasn't present; and to never, ever, give up. The power of conviction would eventually set me free, but first I would have to learn a horrible lesson about the power to convict.

Growing up, we didn't have very much. We were poor, living in the land of plenty. In fact, I felt like I was living on an island, which I know sounds strange given that I was literally living elbow-to-elbow among suffocating masses of people, squeezed into one dilapidated housing project after another. It was rarely quiet, and there were times when I felt like I was drowning in the noise from the cranking of city life around me, made all the more impenetrable by the hum of traffic on I-91–a major highway that stretches from Connecticut's coast to Canada, that was practically pushed into the projects where I lived by the Connecticut River that flows steadily alongside it.

My older brother, Willie, and my younger brother Dennis and I were raised by my mother–a single woman earning minimum wage and working hard to make ends meet. My Mom carried with her the stress of a hard life, along with an unshakable faith in God. Life was not easy for my mother, and I somehow knew that. My mother just didn't have the time to do it all, which meant that I was on my own a lot. At the time I never took it as a negative–like feeling sorry for myself because I didn't have my parents around. It was just the way things were, so I learned how to take care of myself, especially on the streets, which would serve me very well later in life. Even as a little kid, I started to develop my own code–the James Tillman Rules for Survival. While I am outgoing and one who likes to connect, I also like to quietly observe, and I learned a lot by watching people. I quickly noticed that those who were well respected carried themselves a certain way–I could see it in the way they held their head high, how they looked at people, how people looked at them, in the tone of their voice and in the power of their words–their words meant something–they didn't just blab on about nothing. So I began to pay attention to how I carried myself.

I always felt like I had to look after my younger brother, Dennis, but at the same time I was a kid, and I felt that conflict between wanting to do my own thing and watching out for him. Dennis was such a good kid, so I really didn't have to look after him very much– just check in on him and make sure he was okay. I think the process of caring for him became the second part of my developing code: take care of the little guy, because everybody matters. In this case, it meant

Dennis, but I think I was, and still am, always on the lookout for the "little guys" of the world. Armed with those two rules, a sense of curiosity and a desire to connect with others, I began to explore the mean streets of Hartford, Conn.

Because we lived in cramped confines, I loved being outside at the local parks, like Keney Park, where I would play pretty much anything–basketball, paddle tennis, even horseshoes. There were good times, but things could change quickly and unexpectedly. One minute you're lost in a game, and then a fight breaks out, or some dudes come by looking for trouble, and then all hell breaks loose. When I was a kid, I felt like I had to be on guard most of the time–it was hard to settle down and just play.

I never really understood how different things were for me until I had a chance to experience life outside of the city. When I was a young boy, I think I was around 10, we went to visit my cousins, who lived in a house in the suburbs. My cousins had a father and a mother, which was something of a luxury to me. Each of the kids had their own bedrooms–big ones–and they had a nice kitchen, a living room and even a private yard. Man, I thought this was the coolest thing I had ever seen. We weren't there long–it was just a quick visit, but to this day I can remember the feeling of peace and tranquility when I walked in the house. I stood in the front hall, unremarkable by today's standards, looking around in amazement, my heart racing and my mind wandering. How big was this place? I bet I could play hide and seek and never be found. The walls, clean and bright, felt comforting, not confining. The space opened up, there were choices–you could go one way or another, up or down. There was a certain feel to the place–and it was a good one, because it was more than a house, it was a home. I loved that feeling of home, and I spent years dreaming about living that kind of life, where you didn't have to worry about fighting and surviving, where you could have the luxury to relax and play; where you only worried about the plumbing or the landscaping, not the kids outside gang banging or selling drugs; where you could be in a home that you could call your own.

After my voyage into suburbia, I took advantage of every opportunity to experience life outside the city. My Middle School had a tutoring program, arranged through our Church, that enabled us to go to a Church in the suburbs for a day as a part of an exchange program. So we would go to Avon or Simsbury–beautiful towns just outside of Hartford–get tutored, then have dinner with a different family each week. I was always blown away by how much stuff these kids had, and how peaceful the environments were. Sometimes after tutoring, we'd spend the rest of the day playing with the kids, and then we would have dinner together. I loved those experiences, but there was one that stood out.

After finishing dinner, I was admittedly taking my time to pack my things and get ready for the trip home. Already feeling a little sad, I was kind of quiet and pulled in when the Mom's voice yanked me out of my solitary state. "James," she said softly, repeating herself to be break through to me. "James, here honey, we want you to have this," she said, handing me a freshly baked cupcake. "Thank you very much," I said sincerely, feeling tentative, as if I was holding a priceless jewel. I sat in the back seat on the ride home feeling conflicted, staring at the cupcake. I had this overwhelming feeling of wanting to inhale it–just shove it all down my throat in one giant bite, but then another part of me wanted to savor it, for weeks if I could. It was like a work of art, the frosting heaped on top and gently dripping over the edge, almost inviting me to taste it, and the soft cake below practically crushing under its weight. It was such a luxury for me to have this cupcake, so I sat there almost paralyzed, staring at it. Maybe I would eat a little bit and save it, I thought, but where would I hide it? Surely my brothers would find it, and then I'd have nothing–I'd never get this cupcake back again. I knew what I had to do. I gave it one last longing look to store it in my memory, and then ripped the paper off and shoved it mercilessly into my mouth. It was awesome–sweet doughy ecstasy. The kids in the suburbs didn't realize how lucky they were to have so much; to have the houses they had, to live where they lived, to have had two parents, and, of course, to be able to eat things like cupcakes. I began to realize how different our lives were.

On another voyage into the suburbs, I connected with a family through a Church program, and they invited me to come live with them for two weeks during the summer. They welcomed me like I was a part of their family. The father taught me how to buy food and budget my money–bread back then cost 10 cents–times were certainly different! I remember going to the movies to see Willy Wonka with them and we had a ball eating popcorn and talking about the movie. But those good times always had to end when I crossed the city lines and went back to my island.

The summer before I went to 7th grade, I spent some time at the Ethel Walker School in Simsbury, Conn. They held summer programs that allowed kids from the city, like me, the chance to experience life on their campus. I played basketball, hung out with other kids and I really loved it, but a conversation I had with a science teacher illuminated what I was dealing with back then. I was playing ball outside one afternoon, and I kind of owned the court that day. As I walked off the court, smiling, slapping backs and feeling really good, the teacher pulled me aside for a private conversation. "James, why do you do so well here, but so poorly back at home?" It was a great question, especially coming from him, because he wasn't just any science teacher, he was my science teacher in my public school, who also spent time at Ethel Walker during the summer. I fumbled for a bit, because I didn't know how to answer his question, but he was right, there was something different about the experience at Ethel Walker–maybe it was the setting, maybe it was the teachers, maybe it was me? I'm not sure. But then I thought about it, and my answer probably isn't much of a surprise—it's kind of a sad fact about inner-city public schools. "Back home, we only have a science book, and you talk about science, but the kids aren't listening and it's loud, and you can't be heard and it's hard for me to follow. But out here, they have new science books, a science lab with Bunsen burners and Erlenmeyer Flasks and Florence Flasks and I can take what we talk about in the book and try things. Science isn't just something on a page, it's real and you can teach me things in ways you can't back home." He nodded his head in agreement. "It's impossible for me to be bored here," I continued. "There's so much to do and so much to learn and all of the kids are into it, so it's cool." This conversation would help validate the third part of my ever-growing code: keep your mind engaged. Learning is really important, and it doesn't always have to come from a book. It was exciting to experience these things, not just read about them. I bent glass, learned about the different instruments and the education came to life—it really excited me. That experience at Ethel Walker made me realize something I didn't share with a lot of people: I loved to learn.

I excelled on the basketball team at Ethel Walker, but when the awards were given out at the end of the summer, I learned a hard life lesson. I was clearly the MVP of the team, but the coach gave the award to someone else, and suddenly all that hard work kind of felt hollow, because I knew I had earned that trophy. Instead of being recognized as the MVP, I was awarded a consolation prize—a $15 gift certificate to McDonalds for being the Most Valuable Player in the last game of the season. That was my first lesson in the politics of life—that sometimes you're not judged based on the merits but based on who you are and where you're from, and it helped reinforce in me the lifeblood of my developing code—that as I was judged I shouldn't judge others and that I needed to hold onto my own views about what is right and wrong. I saw in the awarding of the trophy that the process wasn't fair, and it broke my spirit and it actually turned me away from basketball for a while, a game I loved. It was a lesson I would learn throughout my life, and later during my trial: that people will let you down and do things that aren't right for their own reasons. I also learned that when bad things happen, there are some people who seek to do good—to engage in what I like to call random acts of kindness. You see, much to my amazement, my science teacher awarded me his own trophy—one that he made up to reward my passion for science. "James, you did well this summer and I'm proud of you," he said handing me a certificate that he made up. I was so grateful. It wasn't the basketball trophy I knew I earned, but it was something special nonetheless. While I walked away from there with a lesson in right and wrong and how some people handle situations, maybe the most important thing I took from the experience was a love and respect for education. I realized that no matter who you are or where you're from, if you have a good teacher with the right tools and you're given that chance, you have a shot at learning. Sadly, a lot of kids, like me, never get that chance. I went back to public school and summarily drown. I did what I had to do to coast through High School, but college was a luxury I couldn't afford. I basically checked out on my education, and I regret that. At the time, I just didn't believe in the value of a college education, or much else for that matter.

So, as the 1980s brought the Reagan Revolution and "Morning in America," Hartford still lay crippled, and I hit her streets armed with a high school education, a desire to work, but not a lot of hope. I worked hard and did the best I could to get by, but I also played hard, and there were some times when I got out of control and I used my fists to make my point. I got into some fights, and I'm not proud of that. I also got busted for driving while intoxicated. I wish I could have made better choices and been a better role model for Dennis, but I always looked at the trouble I got in as the price I paid for living where I lived. Sure, I got dragged down to the police station, fingerprinted, booked and released, but I never saw those incidents as being anything more than part of the natural cycle of life in the projects. I certainly didn't think at the time that the fights would end up being the precipitating events that would land me in prison for over 18 years.

I never realized until much later how growing up in Hartford, a broken city struggling to find its way, and the contrast of the luxurious life others had in the suburbs, would have so much influence on the events that led to my wrongful conviction. But these experiences also instilled in me, in ways I also never appreciated until much later, an unshakable resolve to believe in myself.

Chapter 2

AN UNIMAGINABLE CRIME

T hursday January 21, 1988. It was another day at the car wash for me–a day like any other–but a night that would dramatically change two lives forever. To say that I love cars is an understatement. There is something special about how they're put together, and about what they represent. You can tell a lot about a person by the car they drive and how well they take care of it. My job probably didn't amount to much for most folks, but it was important to me because I took great pride in taking care of the cars. In fact, the hardest part of the job for me was not being able to spend a lot of time cleaning and polishing them. If I could, I would have spent hours on each car, rather than seconds. I wasn't a bank manager or the head of a company. I was one of those guys that most people, busily caught up in their daily lives, never think twice about. My job involved getting into the car after it went through the automatic wash, cleaning and drying it quickly, hopping out and sprinting into the next one. More cars meant more money, so we moved quickly, and that meant I got lots of dings and scrapes on my hands. My work was physical, but I earned a paycheck and I enjoyed it. In fact, the owner of the car wash used to tell me that if he had more people like me, he would be a millionaire, because I cared so much about my work.

At the time I was 26 and living at my Mom's house in the projects, but spending a lot of time at my girlfriend's house, or hanging out with one of my friends. I kind of bounced from place to place a lot when I was younger, so it wasn't unusual for me to crash at a friends house, though the police would later view it with suspicion.

My buddy lived in the projects, too, and I hit his house after work because I promised that I would take him to the car wash in the morning and introduce him to my boss. I have always had an easy time getting along with people, and so asking my boss for a job for someone else was kind of a natural thing for me to do, and I was happy to do it. So as I walked into his house, grabbed a beer and threw myself on the couch, a young white woman left her job at a major corporation in downtown Hartford to meet some friends for drinks at a popular restaurant. My friend and I pounded a few beers, played cards and watched TV. I slept in a bedroom upstairs, and my friend and his girlfriend slept on a pullout couch downstairs. Late at night, as something unimaginable was happening somewhere else in the city, I put my head down on a pillow at my friend's house and fell into a deep sleep.

I am not comfortable sharing the details of a horrible assault, but the facts surrounding it are crucial to my case, so I will share some information from the trial transcripts so that you can judge for yourself whether my conviction was justified. The woman said goodbye to her friends, and at 12:45 a.m. walked a few blocks to her car–a two-door Camaro, which was parked in a poorly lit outdoor parking lot near her office. She opened the door, sat in the driver's seat, and started to close the door. Suddenly, a man jerked-open the door, punched her in the face and then repeatedly beat her in the face. After he beat her, he pushed her over to the passenger's side of the car. She tried to get out the passenger's side door, but the attacker reached over her, slammed the door closed and then beat her a second time. He drove the car to a nearby parking lot where she endured the most inhuman of experiences–she was savagely raped. He tried to get away in her car, but he had trouble driving it–apparently he couldn't drive a manual stick-shift car, so he abandoned the car and ran away on foot (which is why they assumed the attacker lived in that neighborhood–my neighborhood). It is an unthinkable crime. It's hard to even write these words, but if there are lessons to be learned from my case, it's important to understand that she was physically beaten in the eyes, because her entire case against me came down to one thing: what she saw with her eyes–eyewitness identification. Is seeing, believing? Can we say, with conviction, that what we see, especially under stress, is worthy of conviction? Should our convictions be based on what we see, or is there more to it? My freedom depended on the answers to these questions.

Chapter 3

A SIMPLE OVERSIGHT

J ames, wake up. Wake up," my friend rattled me.

"What? Huh?" I said, shaking myself out of the haze of sleep.

I looked at my watch.

"Oh damn," I said to myself. I was overwhelmed with that panicky feeling almost all of us experience at one point in life—I overslept.

This is something I told the police but I have never admitted publicly, because I am embarrassed. Those who know me, then and now, know that I am reliable and hard-working. On that night, though—I took advantage of a chance to hang with a friend and relax—and I got lost in the moment. I drank a few beers and it knocked me out, so I woke up late, and a little hung-over. I was so tired that I didn't even hear the kids in the room next to me wake up and get ready for school that day.

I thought it wouldn't look good to ask my boss to hire my friend on a day when I was so late, so I called in sick and told my friend I'd take him another day, something the police later found suspect. I can tell you now that my actions that night were transparent, fluid and natural. As is the case with a lot of young people, one organic moment led to another and to another. One minute we were hanging out and drinking a beer, then we were playing cards, watching TV, laughing, and then having another beer, and before you know it, it's late and I'm buzzed, so I went upstairs and crashed. I never realized that my every action, my every word, from that night would be scrutinized, looked back upon with judgment, with a bias—from the viewpoint that I was lying and that I raped someone, and then all the information was put into that context and not seen for what it was: a simple screw-up.

On the night of the attack, the victim's life was changed forever, and mine was as well. It's just that for me, I spent the next few days as I would any other—blissfully unaware that a series of events were unfolding around me that would change the course of my life forever. Soon I would realize the dark side of the power of conviction rests in one's power to convict.

Chapter 4

TAKEN FROM HOME

The broken-down two-story wood frame apartments were stacked in dreary uniformity, like dominoes, making it hard to tell one from the next. Open the front door and you were greeted by a massive parking lot that stretched out over a city block. Our neighborhood playground was in reality the overflow parking for the nearby office buildings. Open the back door and you were greeted by a rusty old chain link fence, and beyond that a vast expanse of elevated concrete, welcoming the constant flow of trucks and cars on their way to anywhere but where I lived. Yet despite the noise and the people, I felt physically isolated, maybe even confined by my surroundings, because I always felt like I was living in someone else's space. But the sense of isolation was driven more by my mindset, by the fact that we were poor and living in "Section 8" housing–temporary homes made available by the government to people like us who couldn't afford one on our own. We didn't have that sense of permanence that characterized most homes in most neighborhoods. It's like the constant flow of the river ebbed into the fabric of our community: new people, new drugs, new crimes, new forms of trouble, new opportunities–they were flowing in and out constantly.

That's not to say I didn't appreciate my home–I did. My home provided a sense of stability inside the turbulence, and I reveled in the freedom that it provided. My home was a place to touch back to when I went to work; a place where I could hang out with my brother Dennis; a place to enjoy my Mom's cooking; a place where she could sit and quietly read her Bible.

Sheldon Street wasn't our first choice for an apartment. We had actually found a three family house in another part of the city. The house was huge by Section 8 standards, and it reminded us of the home where my mother grew up in Georgia. My mom was determined to provide the same kind of experience that she had–where family meals around a large table were an important tradition. So, we went to a consignment shop and bought furniture for our new apartment that was similar to my grandmother's, including a full-sized dining room table, a china cabinet and a buffet table. We also got a big L-shaped 1970s-era couch for our living room. Having this furniture made me feel really good, and it fit comfortably into our new home. There I sat, on the first day in our new place, just happy and feeling like we finally found a good home. But as I sat there, I heard an unfamiliar sound of scratching coming from inside the walls, like someone was taking an old toothbrush and running it along the drywall. It was a strange noise, and it came in waves, with flurries of sound, and then silence. It was a sound I had never heard before. We called the superintendent, who came over, heard the scratching and flashed a knowing grin. I can vividly remember the scene of horror that followed. He walked over to a corner, bent down, poked a hole in the wall and backed up as a steady stream of the nastiest looking rats I had ever seen came pouring out of the walls. My mom screamed and I recoiled in disgust. As quickly as we were in this place, we were forced out. The house was condemned; the rats would lose their home in the same moment we did. We had to quickly find another place to live, and the apartment at Sheldon Street was really our only option. So we took it, and force-fit our oversized furniture into this much smaller unit–like wedging the metaphorical square peg into a tiny round hole.

I liked to call Sheldon Street a "see through" apartment, because you could open the front door and see right through the entire house to the back door. Once through the front door, you were welcomed into our foyer–a small box of a room that could barely hold more than a few people. A few steps down a narrow hall took you to the entrance of the living room to the left, and then a couple more to the kitchen, nestled tightly into the back corner of the apartment. In between them rested a set of stairs taking you up to three bedrooms, or down to my room in the basement. We wedged the china cabinet and the dining room table into the kitchen, leaving practically no room to walk. If you were cooking and you needed something from the fridge, you had to squeeze yourself around the table and somehow past the china cabinet. If you got wedged into a seat against the wall for dinner, you had to wait for others to get out, or crawl underneath the table. Then when you made it out into the hall, you had to walk around the buffet table. It was tight, sometimes overwhelmingly so, and it wasn't much by most standards, but it was our home.

I absolutely loved my room in the basement. How could I not like having a place all to myself? In addition to the couch, which mom covered in plastic for protection, I had a bed, a dumpy old box of a television, and a kick-ass stereo system, with a receiver, cassette deck and two large speakers sitting on each side of the unit. A sign of the times, I also had a little table on the other side of the couch with my phone and the phonebook on it (we had to look up phone numbers in a book in those days). Because I was literally underground and surrounded by concrete block, the room was cold in the summer and warm in the winter. There was a tiny window near the stairs that was used as a fire escape. I used to climb in and out of it from time to time, because I was afraid of being trapped in the basement during a fire and I wanted to make sure I could get out. I got long panels of fabric–about six feet wide–and hung them from the ceiling to cover the concrete block walls, alternating a light color and a dark color. This also allowed me to hide the pipes and mechanicals and make the space feel more like a room and less like, well, like a prison cell. I had a beige carpet on the floor that we got for free from someone who was throwing it away. There I'd sit, watching TV late into the night, hanging out with my brother Dennis, or chilling alone listening to Earth, Wind & Fire and Michael Jackson. This was my room, and it was pure heaven.

That's where I was that fateful, otherwise unremarkable cold January day. I lay on my couch, wearing my Kangol hat, a comfortable old pair of jeans and a tee shirt, my head propped on a pillow, watching TV and feeling so relaxed I could barely stay awake. It was almost like a waking dream state. My eyes grew heavy and my head sagged, and then snapped quickly back by the inviting smell of steak simmering in peppers and onions floating down the stairs from the kitchen above. Mom was cooking one of my favorites, and my stomach began to growl in anticipation. I was a lucky guy.

As I lay quietly in my room, pure unadulterated hell was conspiring in the parking lot just outside my front door. A small army of cops pulled into the project: Most of them white. All of them armed. All of them, I would learn later, really pissed off. They were on the hunt for a black man who brutally raped a wealthy, white corporate executive. These guys, a cop would later tell me, were ready to explode by the time they came to arrest me. Hartford was in the midst of a crime wave, and these guys were on the other side of a pretty intense spotlight. Sometimes we find ourselves in situations that drive us beyond the limits of what we would normally do. I'd like to think that given the time to investigate my case, none of the cops there would have chosen to be a part of my arrest. Every single cop present could have been the most honorable person you'd ever meet, but put in this situation with a group of people whose only objective was to apprehend what they thought was a very dangerous criminal, and you can appreciate how they might have felt, but you can also see how things had the potential to unwind quickly.

The cops walked up to some kids who were playing in the parking lot, showed them a picture of me and asked where I lived. The kids pointed to our unit, and then nervously backed away. They knew that something bad was going down. The cops huddled together, and then spread out in formation, with one cop taking the lead and walking up to the door and the others fanning out behind him.

Mom was cooking, quietly singing a hymn, the steak and onions rhythmically sizzling in the background. I stretched, about ready to yell up to mom "is dinner ready?" when I was shaken by the thundering sound of pounding on the door. It wasn't a knock, it was an act of brute force.

"*Boom, boom, boom,*" the sounds echoed throughout the house.

I sat up, confused, wondering what the heck that was? Was it a crash? Did something fall? Was Dennis locked out?

More pounding, this time even louder, as if they were standing right next to me in the basement. "Police. Open up," the voices screamed through that cold January day as the slamming on the door continued.

Police? Why are the cops here, I wondered? What is going on? I stood up, more confused than scared, and the first thought that ran through my head was that something happened in the projects and they needed to talk to us. Maybe a neighborhood kid got in trouble. I started to run down the list of possibilities as I slowly walked up the stairs, greeted by the intoxicating smell of my mom's cooking. Part of me wanted to turn towards the kitchen and blow the cops off and chow down, but I figured that whatever was going on, it wouldn't take long and I'd be eating soon.

"Open up, it's the police. Open the door now!" the voice demanded.

I made my way around the buffet table in the hallway and I looked at my mother, now standing in the foyer, perched against the door. I could sense the fear and confusion in her eyes. I walked by her and motioned with my head for her to step back. I approached the door, pounding like a beating heart. "*Bam! Bam! Bam!*" it rhythmically continued.

"Open the door now. This is the police. We have a warrant for Mr. Tillman," the screams echoed from the other side.

I stood there, just flat-out confused, but now really nervous and almost paralyzed with fear as I stared at the door. On my side of the door: peace and tranquility, a comfortable room and home cooking; on the other side: an angry, snarling hungry monster. I could feel my mother's hysteria building behind me, her cries getting louder and louder. I didn't hear what she said—I don't remember it, but I felt it; I felt her panic. I didn't have a formal college education like many others. I was raised on the streets, and I know how to read a situation from just a look in someone's eye, the way their body was positioned, or the sound of their voice. This just felt bad. Something was really wrong.

My mother stepped forward to my left, she cocked her head right to look at me, and then turned the knob. With that slight turn, the door burst open and police officers, guns drawn, stormed into the house. Everything happened so fast.

"Are you Mrs. Tillman?" one cop screamed to my mother. "I'm James' mother," she replied, confused. "Step aside," he said to her, putting himself in between me and my mother, and pushing her down the hall towards the buffet table.

Almost simultaneously, a cop rushed through the door and came straight at me like a lion to its prey. "Are you James Tillman?" he shouted. "Yeah, I am," I said defiantly, but before I could finish my sentence, I was slammed back against the wall. "What are you doing? What's going on?" My mom started screaming hysterically: "Stop! Stop! Please stop! Don't take my boy!"

"Get your hands where I can see them. Get your hands where I can see them!" the cop screamed. The police were yelling, pushing me, there was so much chaos and confusion in that tight space. I defiantly threw my hands into the air.

"You're under arrest," the cop said to me. "What?!? Are you kidding me? I ain't

done nothin' wrong!" There's no way I could be arrested. I hadn't done anything to deserve even a visit from the police. "What the hell is going on? Why you doin' this?" I demanded. I got no response.

My mind raced. I wanted to fight, I wanted to scream. I wanted to run. "You got the wrong guy!" I said again. Then I felt it. The pressure, pushing up against my ribs so hard it forced me to exhale, and reminded me that I needed to shut up. The force was so intense, I started to collapse into myself from the pain of the cold steel police revolver sticking deep into me. I felt like the only thing that stood between me and my life ending in that very moment was my ability to keep cool. Give these guys any reason, I figured, and they'll take me down right here, right now. "Stay cool James," I mumbled to myself. "Stay cool and don't say a damn word."

With that, another cop moved in and flipped me around, pushing my chest and face against the wall, and pulling my hands down behind my back. I could taste the plaster on the wallboard as I was pressed hard against it. One arm was locked into the cuffs, and then the next one yanked over and locked in. The cuffs hurt like hell. One of the cops spun me around, grabbed me under the armpit, and rushed me out the front door. It was over in a matter of minutes, maybe even seconds. I'm sure I was read my rights, but I don't remember it. I'm sure my mother said something, but I can't recall it. I'm sure the neighbors came out and watched me get taken away by the cops, but I have no memory of it. I'm sure I felt a lot of things, but it's too hard to recall much of that experience. In fact, I've tried hard over the last 26 years to forget everything I can about that fateful day, but that feeling of being uprooted and taken away, like a weed tossed out of the garden, that, I just can't forget...

What I do know, what I do remember very clearly, was the feeling that I was a hair's breath away from getting killed that day. I also knew that I was innocent, but nobody, and I mean nobody, wanted to listen to me or hear that I could be innocent. As far as they were concerned, they got their guy. My torment was their relief.

My head pushed down, I was shoved into the back seat of the police car. The cops then got in the front and slammed the doors. Soon we were rolling out of the parking lot. As we pulled out, I stared back at my house, and I felt a panic. In the commotion, I forgot to grab my wallet. How was I gonna get home later if I didn't have money for a cab? Would the cops give me bus fare? Would one of the cops give me a ride home? Would my mom come get me or would she be too upset? How was I going to get home for that steak dinner? That's all I could think about, because there wasn't any way in the world that I could even imagine that from this exact moment on, I would not taste freedom, I would not step foot in my home again for over 18 years.

Chapter 5:

PRESUMED GUILTY

The day I was arrested, I was taken to one police station where I sat and sat and sat, bored and hungry, with no information about what was going on. Then after a few hours or so, I was hauled out and taken to the main police headquarters in downtown Hartford. I was put in a room–nothing remarkable, it looked like a small conference room, but it had a reflective mirror on one wall. I knew the police were looking at me through that mirror as I sat there alone, waiting, not really sure what was going on. I was just so darn confused. Did one of my friends do something? How does this work? What's gonna happen? Man, I didn't know no lawyers, but even if I did, I could never afford one and I wouldn't know how to get one.

I sat there for what felt like days. It could have been 10 minutes or 10 hours–I'm not really sure. It's crazy how your sense of time gets so messed up in situations like this. I really felt like I was going insane. It felt like all the energy from my mind racing about what was going on was building up inside me to the point where I could burst. Finally, a cop walked in, and I was almost relieved to see another person…just not this one. He looked irritated to be there, like I was wasting his time. He sat down and got right to the questions.

"Mr. Tillman, are you drinking or using drugs?" he asked, like he was pissed off that he even had to ask me.

"No. I'm not," I replied clearly, making direct eye contact, feeling angry.

"Take off your shirt," he said with an angry tone in his voice. I hesitated. I was embarrassed. He stared at me. We were like fighters sparring, although I knew that I was fighting with both hands tied behind my back, but it didn't mean I had to make this easy for him. After all, he was standing between me and my steak dinner. "Mr. Tillman, take off your shirt," he demanded. I gave in, and I took my shirt off.

"Stand up and turn around," he said evenly. I stood up and turned around, feeling humiliated. I realized they were checking me for scratches and bruises. I didn't have any, and the whole process was embarrassing. I sat down and put my shirt back on.

"Show me your hands," the cop snapped. I put my hands out, and he used an instant camera to take pictures of them. My hands were a little dinged from my work in the car wash–a small scar on the ring finger of my right hand and a bruise near the knuckle on the middle finger of my left hand, but nothing major. No cuts or scars that would come from the result of a brutal beating.

I wasn't technically arrested right away–I sat in a room and the police came in and out. I don't remember most of the questions because they weren't really asking me anything serious, until a detective came in. I could tell by the way he carried himself that he was the one in charge.

"Where were you the night of January 21st?" he asked me.

I paused. I had to think about it for a minute.

"I was with my friend and his girlfriend—we were playing cards and hanging out," I said. I gave him their names and the address.

"That scar on your hand is fresh—where did you get it?" he asked me.

"No, it isn't officer," I replied declaratively. "I got this from work—I get these things all the time moving cars."

The detective left, and I sat there alone, again. I looked up and saw men moving behind the glass, even though I don't think I was supposed to be able to see them, I definitely saw them. Then the detective came in asked me again where I was on the night of the 21st. I told him, again, that I was at my friend's house. "Stop lying to me," he shouted, growing angry and intense, leaning forward and getting in my face. I knew he was trying to rattle me, so I stayed calm.

"I'm not lying," I said in a matter of fact way.

"Do you know that a woman was beaten very badly a few nights ago? She was beaten so bad that she might lose her eye. Did you know that, Mr. Tillman?" the detective asked. "No, I didn't know that," I replied as if I was reading the phone book. I honestly didn't, but beyond the substance of any of my answers, I was determined not to let this guy shake me up. We were playing a game, and I wasn't going to lose.

"Yeah, Tillman, well, we've got your fingerprints at the scene," the detective said to me concretely, as if he wasn't the one lying directly to my face. How could that be true? I knew he was lying, and in fact when it came to the trial it would be proven that that statement was in fact, a lie. My fingerprints were not on the car, or the victim's briefcase, or in any way at the crime scene.

The detective leaned close to me, like he was about to give me a secret tip on a stock. "You'd better confess," he said, almost in a whisper. "This person you attacked. Her father called the Chief of Police, and that Dad, he's a big man around here, so you may as well confess now and get it over with."

"I didn't do it," I replied in a matter-of-fact tone.

"Confess, Tillman!" the cop demanded. "Admit what you did!" he shouted.

"I'm not confessing to anything because I didn't do anything," I shot back.

The cop put a folder on the table in front of me. "Open it up," he said. I did, not knowing what to expect, but knowing it wouldn't be good. It was a picture of the victim, her face beaten. It was horrible to look at and it made me angry to see her in pain, and it made me even angrier that they thought I could do this. I wanted to slam the table, scream, turn it upside down and run. I was filled with rage. 'Yeah, this is awful for her, but it sucks for me right now, too,' I thought to myself.

"She's going to lose that eye," the detective said to me, pointing to the picture.

"I didn't do it," I said, with the same measured tone, the same cadence, standing firm. "Why don't you go find the person who did?" I asked. I got no reply.

Why are they so focused on me when I have an alibi and I'm innocent? I kept asking myself that question, and I couldn't figure out the answer. I couldn't understand why they were so sure I did it, when the facts clearly showed I did not. How did I get here? Here's how it happened: The victim was shown a photo array–an organized group of pictures. The detective put the pictures together thinking that one of the people shown in the pictures may have committed the crime. That was, to my knowledge, the focus of the investigation. The victim, sitting with a social worker but not the policeman, looked at those pictures and saw nothing. When the cop came back in the room, having nothing else prepared and organized, he then pulled out what is, in essence, a photo album containing mug shots of people from the inner-city who had been arrested. He gave her the book and left the room again. She flips a page, sees my picture, and starts to shake and cry. The detective comes back in the room, and she tells him that I'm the one who raped her, but, interestingly, that I "look different." He searches, finds a different photo of me that's smaller and in black and white, and therefore harder to distinguish details. He shows the second photo to her, and she confirms that I'm the person who raped her. And that's pretty much the extent of the police investigation that led to my arrest and incarceration. Next thing you know, I'm sitting in this chair and being told to confess to something I didn't do.

I later learned that the vast majority of rape cases involve either prior sexual abuses or a relationship with the victim. I had no prior sexual abuses, nor did I ever meet the victim or have a relationship with her—we were living in two totally different worlds. Turns out the guy who committed the crime did have prior sexual assaults. For such a serious and awful crime, I was arrested based on one thing: what a woman who was savagely beaten thinks she saw in a picture—a picture of me taken when I was younger.

Without coming across as impolite on matters of race, if I took 100 2x3 inch pictures of people of a certain race and put them on a table in front of a person of a different race and told that person to find one person, I'm not sure the correct person could be picked with 100 percent certainty. Put another, more direct way: sometimes a lot of young black men do look alike, especially when a picture is so small that you can't see any distinguishing features.

It seemed everything about my case came down to that one picture, and I have been haunted by so many questions. What did the policeman really say when he gave her the pictures? How was the picture placed in front of her? Was mine separated, maybe pushed more forcefully in front of her? Were all the pictures picked randomly? Did he react non-verbally when she picked my photo? Were comments made during the process? How were the pictures organized and presented to her? What was the basis for selecting the pictures? Was she told that it could be me but it could not be me? That one fleeting moment of time ricocheted like a domino, starting a cascade of injustice that would steamroll through the next 18½ years of my life.

According to the Innocence Project, eyewitness misidentification is the leading cause of wrongful convictions nationwide. It has played a role in over 75% of the wrongful convictions they have helped overturn, including mine. But back in 1988, those statistics didn't matter. In fact, the only stat that mattered was that someone was arrested and convicted. A horrible, unthinkable crime had occurred, in a city that was very publicly trying to rebuild its image. Someone -- anyone -- had to be held accountable. It mattered more that I could have been guilty than that I was innocent. It was only my life, after all, and I was one of those people that the Other Connecticut forgot, so what did it matter to them?

The night dragged on. I was sitting in the interrogation room alone, tired, hungry and scared, realizing that this was serious. There were times when I thought I might go crazy. Then the police would come back in, hit me with some information, and then leave. All the evidence they said they had tying me to the crime—they had it wrong. They had to know it, but they kept pushing.

"Tillman, you work with cars, You know how to drive if stick shift." "So what," I thought. "So do about a million other guys."

As much as they kept getting in my face, I gave it back to them, and never broke. I didn't have to worry about what I said, because I had the truth on my side, so I never wavered. While I never admitted guilt, I can understand how someone might break down after endless hours of interrogations. There were definitely points where I would have said yes if it would have gotten me out of that situation.

Sitting there, your whole sense of reality changes. You almost start to believe the things they're telling you, or you get tired and trip up and then they twist your words around. The whole thing was a mess.

I'm a big believer that you should act in private the same way you act in public, for nobody can fully hide from God's eyes. Another part of my code was forming right before my eyes. If this simple standard were held for all of us, I'm not sure the police who interrogated me would want the world to see the way they acted with me in private. How could they lie to me telling me my fingerprints were found at the crime scene to coerce a confession just to close a case? What if that same amount of effort was spent trying to find the person who actually committed the crime? What they did to me that day was flat out wrong. While I forgive them, it is something that they will have to reconcile as they hopefully look to change the way they do business. Their lies and poor police work cost me 18 years of my life.

The detective kept coming back to my hands—that was their big piece of evidence that proved that I committed the crime. I'm not a cop or a lawyer, but I do know something about fights. I know what your hands look like after a fight—and my hands certainly didn't look like they were involved in a fight. The cop kept telling me that I beat her so badly that she might lose her left eye, and I'm right- handed and yet there was nothing on my right hand, on either hand for that matter, that would indicate that I beat someone so badly they would lose an eye. In fact, the scratch on my right hand was pretty small—and if I had been in a fight four days earlier, that small scratch would not only still be fresh, but it would be substantial. I really didn't think about those kinds of details at that moment because never in my wildest dreams did I think I was going to be put away for years or months or even days. I just sat there, alone, in shock, answering the same questions again and again, thinking I must have convinced them that they were focusing on the wrong person, until finally it seems they convinced themselves that they had the right one.

The detective came in the room while I sat there nervously tapping my left leg. "Mr. Tillman, you are under arrest. You have the right to…" I didn't hear another word. My mind went blank. A surge of adrenaline ran through my body as if I was electrocuted. "Oh my God," I said to myself. "This is really happening! I can't believe it. No!! I didn't do it!" I just kept repeating the same thing again and again: "I can't believe this is happening."

Injustice fell on me like rain, and no matter where I went or what I did, I could not find shelter. On Tuesday January 26, 1988, just five days after a woman was brutally raped in Hartford, Connecticut, I was forced out of my home in handcuffs, paraded and down my front steps–steps I ran up and down a thousand times. Here I sat in police headquarters, about to be shipped off to jail. I couldn't get my head around what was happening. I was hungry and I wanted to go home.

As those first hours and days unfolded, all I remember thinking about was how much I wanted Mom's steak. I knew that whatever it was they thought I did, I didn't do anything wrong, and so I just kept thinking to myself: 'when am I going to get a chance to eat mom's steak?' I could smell the simmering onions. I could hear the sizzling of the steak cooking. I could see my Mom standing next to the oven, quietly singing. I thought of that steak dinner often in prison. I told myself that if I ever got out, I would appreciate every home cooked meal, because you never know when it might be your last. For the next 18½ years, I could only live with the thought of the meal that might have been. It was a meal I thought about, dreamed about, longed for. It was my own "Last Supper."

We live in a system of laws, but those laws are enforced by, and applied to, real people. People make mistakes. Sometimes, we hold onto our convictions so strongly that we forget that we all are imperfect beings, and the humility, the honesty, that is required to acknowledge our imperfections is often lost in the arrogance of those who hold power. There is a difference between holding onto what we believe about ourselves and what we hold to be true about someone else; there is a fine line separating the power of conviction form the power to convict.

I was about to be tested—I was heading deep into the darkest parts of hell, but unaware of it—as many of us are when we face tough times. One moment we're fine, and the next everything falls apart. Thankfully in that moment, I wasn't aware just how hard the next 18 years would be, and so I wouldn't have to question whether or not I could make it—the only thing I had going into that prison was my belief in myself.

Chapter 6

MORGAN STREET MADNESS

I was put in a holding cell at the Morgan Street Jail in Hartford, where I waited for my appearance before the Judge. The jail was notorious for its cramped and inhospitable conditions. In fact, a group of doctors hired by the Department of Corrections issued a scathing report in December 1987, calling for the prison to be closed. I entered Morgan Street a short while later.

My cell was unusually small, even by prison standards. Imagine walking down the street and jumping into a manhole and landing in a small room with bars on one side and concrete all around you. A room so small that you and your cellmate couldn't stand in the cell at the same time—one of you had to be on the bed for the other to walk around. That was my reality. Taken from the streets, and transplanted into what was, in essence, a cave. A tiny, smelly, dark, horrible cave.

The jail was meant to house people temporarily before trials. Most inmates stayed at Morgan for about 10 days before being transferred.

I was there for more than a month. I was so rattled by my new surroundings that it was all I could do to keep my sanity–never mind prepare for a trial. While I live by the James Tillman code, I quickly learned that prison has its own code. Put simply, pedophiles and snitches are not tolerated, and rapists are held a level above that, which meant that I walked into prison, innocent, with a big target on my back. The punishment? Depending on how you carry yourself and who can vouch for you, you're either harassed, beaten and tormented, or in some extreme cases, raped or killed. Sure enough, almost immediately, my cellie tried to set me up. Within a day, I heard him whispering to people. "Tillman's a rapist," which meant that people were going to come after me. He didn't want a rapist for a cellie because of the attention it might bring him, so he wanted me beaten up or moved. I knew I would be a target until I could prove that I was someone who should be left alone.

Most who were imprisoned at Morgan St. posted bail and waited for trial in the comfort of their own homes, but not me. I couldn't afford bail, not to mention a lawyer. I couldn't afford anything. So, the first lesson I learned about our justice system seems almost naïve: money makes a difference. It's funny: prison is full of every type of person–rich, poor, young, old, black, white, etc. Once inside, class distinctions pretty much fade away. You're all wearing the same suits and the same stripes, living in the same sized cells–prison is the great equalizer, but justice is not. Money plays a huge role in the justice system. Money can buy you luxuries I could never afford: an exceptional lawyer, maybe even a team of lawyers, experts, people who have the time to focus on you and give you the best possible chance to make your case. Money can buy you a variety of tests that can help to prove your innocence. Money also has a more subtle influence in the justice system, at least as I experienced it: money buys you credibility. I really never looked at my case in strictly racial terms as much as it was a case of economics–rich vs. poor; wealthy powerful, suburbanites vs. poor, powerless inner-city man. Granted, there have been cases where high profile rich people have suffered major credibility problems, but they're usually not against poor people plucked off the streets of the inner city–they're usually against their own kind. Would my case have been different had the police driven up to a 10,000 square foot home in the wealthy section of West Hartford that night and stuck a gun to the head of the child of someone who owned a dozen car washes around the Hartford suburbs? We'll never know. I'm certainly not saying that wealthy people are bad–not by any means. I simply wonder how my case would have been different had I had access to some of the world's best lawyers as I did during my work with the Connecticut Innocence Project?

There I sat in the Morgan Street jail. Arrested for a crime I did not commit. I didn't sleep well there. I kept people at bay by carrying myself with a certain look: touch me and I will break you in half, but it meant that I was constantly on guard. On the surface, I was a volcano, but deep down I was scared. I missed my home and my family. It's hard to explain what happens to your brain in a place like this, but strange things happen. You go from thinking about lots of things–how am I going to clean this car, where am I going for lunch, should I watch the ballgame tonight? One minute you breathe fresh air. You look out your window and see the sun. You know what day it is. Then the next minute, all that changes. You spend your days thinking about the trial. You stare at the same wall hour after hour after hour. You turn a corner and you worry about getting the shit kicked out of you. It's boring, frustrating and monotonous, but every moment is also filled with fear, anxiety or raw emotion. You go from living a life filled with choices to a life where there are few choices left.

One of the things I learned in retrospect is that what you physically do with your life changes the way you think. I tried to hold onto all the things that were familiar to me before I went in, like the sounds and the smells of daily life, but it was hard. I kept believing that I would be in the comfort of my own home soon, and I awoke the next day believing, firmly, that they would realize they made a mistake and I would be freed. I held onto that hope, but it faded fast, because the only thing I literally experienced was lying on a tiny cot staring at lifeless walls. It was hard to feel hope among such hopelessness.

I went from living day-to-day with a long view of life to living minute-by- minute. I wasn't mentally prepared to serve a week in prison, never mind 18+ years. Rather, I was focused on going home that day. Every morning I woke up I'd think: is today the day I'm going home? So each day brought emotional highs and lows for me. As another day passed and I was still in that tiny cell, I grew frustrated, but held onto the hope that the next day might bring my release. It was like I was playing the lottery, thinking that tomorrow I would win, when in reality I never even bought a ticket. I guess I started to become delusional as a matter of survival. I continually brushed aside the temporary inconvenience of prison, telling myself that I would be home soon; that this horrible experience was only temporary, but then in the next moment I realized it wasn't, and that I was stuck. It was like I was schizophrenic, and then the really crazy things started happening. I began to hallucinate.

During one two-day period, my cellie was moved and I was alone in the cell. It was at once awesome because I was finally alone, but once alone, things got a little freaky. My first night without a cellie, my first night alone in prison, I lay back on my cot, my mind racing, my body urging it to shut up so I could get some sleep. Crazy stuff just started flying through my mind at light speed. I pictured the interrogation room. My room in the basement. Then I'm playing ball at Ethel Walker as a kid. I'm playing in the park with Dennis, and then a cop is screaming in my face. Then I'm eating a cupcake in the suburbs. Finally it slowed down, and I lay there in a moment of unusual peace. Just then, I had that weird feeling—the one you get when you're walking upstairs and you're sure someone is behind you. I felt a rush of adrenaline come over me.

And then I felt someone in the cell with me. I could feel a presence next to me. I could hear someone breathing. Someone is definitely here, I thought. I sat up, looked around. I saw nothing, but I felt it–something, someone was definitely in that room. Everyone said Morgan Street was haunted, and I wondered, "could that be true?" That feeling came from a finely tuned sense that one develops in prison–you just kind of know when danger is imminent. I could feel it, and it scared the hell out of me. "James are you there?" I heard a faint whisper, but I couldn't quite make out the words. They just hung there, draped around my dark cell. A footstep fell gently, with a shuffle, and then another whisper. "Who's there?" I whispered forcefully. I sat up, stiff, still, in a panic. Was someone in my cell? Is someone here to kill me? I looked around, but saw nothing. I strained my ears, but heard nothing. I slowly eased my head back down, tense, full of fear. It was the middle of the night and everyone was sleeping. I heard another sound–like someone was literally on top of me, but nobody was there. Was it a ghost? Was I going crazy? I started talking to myself in a low whisper. 'James, it's okay, you're here in jail. There's nobody in here with you. It's going to be okay.' I lay there motionless, just repeating 'it's going to be okay,' when I knew it wasn't. So I sat there in a panic, with every atom in my body buzzing a million miles an hour. It was the most frightening moment of my life, and there wasn't a thing I could do about it except lay there and sit with the fear– all night long. I never slept, not even a wink. Finally daylight broke. I heard the familiar footsteps of the guards making their rounds. As one drew close, I walked to the edge of the cell and pleaded.

"Hey, can I talk to a counselor or someone? I had a crazy night. I can't take this."

Later that morning, I heard the sound of the door creak. "Slam," it smacked open, with force. I tensed up and cocked my arm, thinking about how to protect myself. Get behind the bed, I thought, and use it to shield you. I was ready to take this person down if need be, and then

I made eye contact and I cracked a smile. It was a bizarre scene—me, in a violent jail, wearing a prison uniform, tense and ready to kill someone, and standing before me a woman of God, a nun, wearing her uniform—hers by choice, mine by condemnation. She held out her hands, and placed in mine an offering of unconditional love—a Bible. We talked for a little while, but I was too scared and too filled with hate to recognize the gift, and so I took it for what I thought it was: words on a page, pages in a book, and a book that would help me pass the time, but it wasn't anything more than that.

After she left, I sat there, still feeling unnerved. I grabbed the Bible, read it cover to cover and began to feel a sense of total peace. When I was finished, I put the Bible on my cot and sat there. For the first time in what was a very long time, I felt calm—not the way you might think of calm, like sitting around and taking deep breaths. No, my sense of peace came when my anxiety was replaced by anger, even hatred. I was calm because in my heart I hated everyone and I knew it and allowed myself to feel it. I was in tune with my raw emotion, and it kind of filled me up from head to toe and literally changed the way I carried myself. Now I wore my anger like a coat for my own protection, and it sent a very clear message: 'mess with me and I will snap you like a twig.'

Chapter 7

CONVICTED

I sat in a lifeless jail cell waiting, day after day after day after day, waiting for someone to set me free. Knowing I was innocent, I set my mind on getting to trial, where I was convinced that the truth would finally put an end to this tragic mistake. After nearly 2 years of waiting, my moment finally came on September 11, 1989.

I wanted to hire an attorney to handle my case, but I couldn't afford one, so I had to use the public defender. It goes without saying that I didn't feel like I was a priority for an over-worked, under-staffed Public Defender's Office. As much as I wasn't confident that they really got my case, I didn't sweat it that much because I knew I was innocent and I just believed that the truth would set me free.

The trial began with the selection of the jury. I remember sitting there, in this business-like room with the judge on a platform and people coming in and out and talking a lot saying things I didn't quite follow, thinking that something didn't feel right. I looked at the jury, and thought: these aren't my people; this is not a jury of my peers. After all, I am black, poor and from the City of Hartford, while the jury pool was picked from the wealthy, predominantly white suburbs like West Hartford, Farmington and Avon. The jury looked more like they were peers of the victim than they were related in any way to me.

One of the things often overlooked in trials like mine is the fact that jurors are paid a pathetic amount of money: $10 per day at my trial. Many corporations will provide a full-day's pay for service, but for many of my "peers" jury duty wasn't an option because they couldn't afford to give up a good day's work for 10 bucks. So the very pool of people from which the jury would be selected was skewed before we even began the trial. The deck was already starting to be stacked against me.

No surprise then that when my jury was picked, there were no minorities on the panel. I questioned my lawyer, because this didn't feel right to me. "Is this legit?" I asked him. "How can this be fair? There's nobody like me on that jury, but there are a lot of people like her." My attorney heard me out and said he would talk to someone about it. I know from reading the motions on my appeal that he did talk to the clerk and asked him why there were so few minorities in the jury pool. It's my understanding that he was told that most of the minorities were either in a pool for a trial next door or excused because they had to work. My attorney got his answer, but he never formally objected to this or raised it as an issue in the courtroom to the judge. That oversight would prove devastating to my chance of appeal.

While many who have looked at my trial comment on the racial makeup of the jury having had a major affect on the outcome–the jury was comprised of five whites and one Hispanic–I think the bigger issue was that nobody was from my Island. If there are two Hartfords, as I describe, then everyone on the jury was from the other one. I would have rather had a poor white jury than a wealthy jury of any color. I got a jury that was wealthy *and* white. I sat there during the selection process and one thought kept going through my mind: this is most definitely not a jury of my peers.

Further complicating matters, while outside events aren't supposed to influence my case, my trial came on the heels of a horrific high profile crime—one of the worst in Connecticut history. Daniel Webb, an African American man from the city who was around my age, brutally raped and then killed a white woman—a bank executive—in Keney Park, the park where I played as a kid. The crime occurred a little over two weeks before my trial started at a time when Hartford was desperately trying to rehabilitate its image. I sometimes wonder how much that horrible crime, and the rage many of the jurors must have felt, influenced my case. Was I going to pay for Daniel Webb's sins?

Despite the setback on the selection of the jury, I still had a lot of hope going into the trial that the truth would come out when the facts were presented. I believed in our system of justice, although I knew as a poor black man from the streets that things didn't always go our way. I heard stories of people being railroaded before. As soon as the victim's attorney started and I looked at the jurors faces, I knew it wasn't good. I got a really bad feeling inside that I wasn't going to get a fair shake. More than the way the jurors looked at me, I got this feeling from the way people carried themselves around me. Everyone, except for my family, treated me like I was a convicted criminal, not like a person who was innocent until proven guilty. This cake was already baked. I started to have doubts that the truth would set me free.

The trial started with the victim taking the stand and recalling the events in graphic detail. The circumstances were so horrible, and I could feel people's eyes turn to me with each graphic description of the events, as if to say, 'how could you do such a terrible thing, you monster?' The prosecutor kept motioning to me, looking at me, pointing at me. He was effective in using his body language to connect me to the woman. With each word, I felt more and more uncomfortable. I wanted to jump out of my chair and scream, "I didn't do it! Don't you get it, I didn't do it! It wasn't me!" But it felt to me that the trial was more about me having to prove I wasn't guilty than protecting my innocence. During the end of the prosecutor's questioning, he asked her if she got a good look at her attacker, and she replied by saying that she was bleeding badly, couldn't see out of her left eye and that her right eye was beaten up but that she could see well enough to see who did it. Every time I heard her talk about what happened to her, I grew sick inside, filled with rage. But when I heard her talk so convincingly about it being me, I wondered how she could be so sure that she got a good look at her attacker. I just wanted to explode at her: It wasn't me!! You know it wasn't me! Stop lying!

I decided in writing this book that I would not go into all the details of the trial and the actual crime. However, I do think it's important if we are to learn from this that I raise *some* details because they form the two pillars of evidence in the trial: witness identification and the main forensic evidence—a basic blood test.

In terms of witness identification, the crime occurred in the dark at 12:45 a.m. in a corporation's outdoor parking lot. As mentioned before, the victim got into her car, turned the car on, and then the attacker surprised her, opened the door and punched her in the face—that was the first thing that happened, so it wasn't like she had a good look at the person before the crime was committed, or saw this guy approaching her. After beating her in the face, he pushed the victim to the passenger's side of the car, and she tried to get out. At that point, he reached across her and slammed the door shut and locked it, beating her again. The attacker's fingerprints were on the car door, but it was never made clear enough at the trial that my fingerprints were not on the car.

The pictures used for the basis of the eyewitness identification came as a result of a description the victim gave to the police. Due to the fact that she was in the hospital for three days, she did not meet with the police at the station for three days.

Because the prosecution's case rests almost entirely on eyewitness identification, I want to be careful how I present this, and so maybe it's best to use language from the trial. According to a brief provided by the State of Connecticut, this is how the victim made that crucial identification:

"The victim wanted to make an identification of her assailant, and met with [name deleted], a social worker with the Hartford Police Crisis Unit and with Detective [name deleted] of the Hartford Police Department on January 25, 1988. At headquarters, Detective first brought her a set of Polaroid pictures of black men, but the victim did not recognize any of the individuals. The Detective then handed her a book of police photographs. He left the victim with [name deleted], and, shortly thereafter, the victim recognized a picture of her attacker, which caused her to shake and cry. She told [name deleted] that she recognized her attacker, but that he looked younger in the picture. Detective came back in and said he would try to get a more recent photo. The first picture was dated April 1983. Detective returned with another picture of the defendant taken in June 1987. The victim identified this picture and had no doubt that it was the man who had attacked her."

With a case resting on eyewitness identification, the victim looked through instant camera pictures and did not find anyone, was given a book of pictures with minimal instructions, leafed through a few pages and then stopped at my photo. So the detective brought her a more recent picture, put it in front of her and asked, "is that him?" I'm no lawyer or expert, but I'm told that is not the way eyewitness identification should be handled. This process just doesn't seem fair to me. I always wondered what happened at that moment. In fact I spent years wondering: did the person showing her the picture steer her in any way? Could the police detective have made eye contact at the moment she looked at my picture? Or moved in his chair or made an audible sound? Something that would reinforce her decision? There seemed at some level to be some uncertainty. In fact, at trial, the Detective testified as follows: "I told her that I was going to show her photographs of black males. And I asked her to study the photographs, remembering that people can shave, they can grow beards, we may not have a photograph of the person exactly as he appeared. So I just told her to study the faces. If she saw the person, tell us. If she saw someone that was not perfect— had similar features, point those out so we know what we're looking for." In my view, his words gave her permission to make a mistake, in a case whose foundation was based on not making a mistake about precisely what she saw.

Even at the moment when she pointed at me during the trial, she said I looked different than I supposedly did the night of her attack, but that was chalked up to my natural aging rather than it not being the right person. My attorney didn't press her very much in response to what she actually could see that night, I think because it was such a sensitive topic and so difficult to talk about. Had this been a street brawl, I'm sure my attorney would have probed every facet of the case, but because it involved the violent rape of an innocent woman, things weren't pushed too hard. There was so much focus on the victim of the attack, I don't think a lot of people even thought that there could be a second victim sitting in that court room during the trial. My attorney did ask her specifically about what she remembered about the attacker. She said she was able to look at the profile of his face when he reached across to shut the passenger door. Did she remember any distinctive features? Any scars? Moles? Gold teeth? Any marks on the face? Understandably for someone who had been through such a horrible nightmare, the answers were all no. She couldn't remember anything specific about her attacker, but she was still certain, in looking at a Polaroid picture, that I was the guy.

What I found very curious and interesting is that the victim did not give a description of her attacker to the detective until AFTER she made the eyewitness identification through the picture. The police the night of the attack, I learned, had a general description of the attacker, but the detective in charge of the investigation didn't talk to the police who were at the scene on the night of the crime until after the victim made her identification. The detective admitted during the trial that they just gave the victim books of people who committed crimes or lived in the area where the crime occurred. The police did not take a description, find pictures that matched the description, and then show them to the victim in some kind of random, standardized order. In addition, the brief description she gave the two officers at the scene was different than the one she gave to the detective days later, but the discrepancies were never talked about or accounted for before I was arrested. For example, the length of sideburns, the kind of hat, the height of the attacker were described differently to police the night of the attack and then days later at the police station. And when the detective showed the victim my second picture, it was a different size–shrunk down and in black and white, so details were hard to determine. Why did it happen that way? In other words, it seems to me that this whole process was messed up and backwards. Was this a police investigation that justified incarcerating a human being?

My attorney did try to raise an objection about the differences between the two police descriptions and how they related to me. For example, the victim told the police her attacker was between 5'7" and 5'10"–I'm 5'5". Sadly, when my attorney pressed the judge on these differences, he said it didn't matter, and so these differences were allowed to stand and my trial went on, with no more challenges to how the photographs were put together and the eyewitness identification made, how the description changed and how the police from the crime scene and the detective who led the charge to arrest me did not work together.

From that moment on, I was screwed because I had no way to counter one of the pillars of their case: eyewitness identification.

The other pillar of the prosecution's case was the forensic evidence. A great deal of time was spent at trial on the use of forensic evidence to prove that I could have been the attacker. Unfortunately for me, DNA testing hadn't been perfected at the time, so the forensic discussion basically boiled down to what are now seen as crude blood tests. The victim's garments were tested for the presence of seminal fluid and blood, and then my blood was drawn. I learned at the trial that the experts were looking for a certain type of "acid phosphates"–an enzyme that is found in seminal fluid. Seminal fluid was found on her pantyhose and dress and there was blood on her dress. Seminal fluid either has or does not have antigens–a chemical found in body fluid. These antigens are secreted in some people and are not in others. So people were broken down into two categories at the time: secretors and non-secretors. I'm a non-secretor with Type A blood. Complicating things, there were two different kinds of seminal fluid found on the victim's clothing. There was seminal fluid on the pantyhose from a non-secretor with Type A blood–someone in my category–but there was also seminal fluid on the dress from a secretor with Type B blood. Which seminal fluid belonged to the rapist? Further complicating things, a rape kit that was collected at the Hospital was never tested. Why? This information was the basis of the forensic evidence used to prosecute me. The prosecutor had an expert testify about the forensics who said that the tests taken showed that I could have been the attacker–we were both non-secretors. What wasn't mentioned was that so could have about 50% of the black male population in Hartford–a wide net to cast in looking for a specific person. The tests showed that it could have been me, not that it was absolutely, positively was me. It was also uncovered in a 2009 article by Peter Neufeld that the person testified inaccurately about the forensic evidence. Among other things, he failed to acknowledge that testing results might have been inconclusive due to degradation of one of my samples.

However, the police were so forceful and effective in their testimony, which was not countered with any experts in my defense, that what now seems questionable was presented and seen as fact at the time.

The more I heard the evidence at the trial, the more confused I got. I saw the holes in their case very clearly, but I didn't get the feeling that the jurors did. I saw the complications about the forensic evidence. Did they? I was confused as to why there was not a lot of discussion about my features as I sat there in the room—only how her description could match an old photo that lacked details. Did they see the problems there, too? The victim said she kicked, punched and grabbed her attacker, yet there were no marks on my face or body. Did that sink in? The attacker spoke to her, but there was not a lot of discussion about my voice, or how it did or didn't compare with the attacker. We were told that the attacker reached across the car and closed the passenger's door, and later during the attack he rummaged through her briefcase. The car was swept for fingerprints, but the brief case was not. Fingerprints were found on the car, but they were not mine, and they were not sent to the state fingerprint identification bureau to match anyone else. Why? There were so many holes in this case, could the jury see that? Or had they formed an opinion and were simply looking for the right facts to back it up, conveniently discarding the rest?

There were eight witnesses for the prosecution: the victim, her husband, and six members of the City and State Police Departments. In addition to me, my attorney called two people in my defense. As mentioned, the night of the rape, I stayed with my friend and his girlfriend. I slept in a room upstairs, her kids slept in the room next to me, and my friend's girlfriend slept on the pull-out couch downstairs. She testified that she saw me that night—my friend and I were hanging out and having a few beers and playing cards; that she was up watching

TV until about 1 a.m., and that there was one set of stairs from the first floor to the upstairs and that I never left the house. She also testified that she saw me sleeping in the bed when she went upstairs to get her kids ready for school the next morning, and that she helped wake me up later that morning. Interestingly, when the detective came to the house to interview my friend, the detective never talked to the girlfriend, despite the fact that she was there that night and she was there while he was conducting the interview. Why?

I sensed from the overwhelming nature of the victim's personal testimony and the power of the police testimony, that things did not look good for me. I sat in my cell after a particularly long day of testimony. "Hey Tillman, how'd it go?" the guy in the next cell asked me. "Not good," I replied quietly. "It's not looking good." "Well…" he said, laughing, "I'm innocent too!" "Shut up!" I screamed back at him, cutting him off.

Throughout the trial I held out hope that they would realize that I was innocent. I hoped they would see the facts, and I would be cleared. More than a grasp of the facts, I hoped the jury would get a fair view of who I was and understand that I wasn't capable of such a horrible crime.

After the closing arguments were made, but before the jury presented its verdict, I was taken to a small room near the courtroom. As soon as my attorney sat down, I knew it was serious. "James, they have a deal for us," he said to me. I leaned forward, curious. Here's my break, it's finally coming. This whole thing was a game of poker. I felt like they knew they didn't have the evidence to justify my conviction and they wanted to find a way out to save face. They're going to set me free. I was pumped up. I leaned forward, with great anticipation, almost hopping in my seat. "What do you mean, 'a deal'?" I asked. He replied like he was reading a grocery list, not like my life lay in the balance. "If you plead guilty, you will be given a sentence of five years. With time served already, you'll be looking at another six months or a year and then you'll be released on probation." Six months. Six lousy months. My attorney is a good person, so I don't want this to come across the wrong way, but to me this was a deal with the Devil. Six months of prison time or potentially decades behind bars, maybe even the rest of my life. I had a choice. Accept the deal, and walk out a free man in six months, or take my chances with the jury. "What do you think, James?" my attorney asked. To me, it was an absolute no-brainer–I didn't have to even think about it, the answer was so crystal clear to me. "No way," I said emphatically. "I'd have to carry the label of a 'convicted rapist' for the rest of my life. I'm not doing that. I didn't rape her. I won't cop to something I didn't do. I'll be going to family birthday parties or holidays and my own family will look at me strange, you know? How will I get a job? How could I live with myself? Taking this deal will mean that I will have to admit to something I'm not. I am not a rapist. I won't do it. I ain't taking the deal." I knew that every time I walked down the street, people would think twice about me. It would be a stain on my character, and a stain on my family's name. How would they deal with it? Would my brother or mother be ridiculed or outcast because of me? But more important than any of this, how could I look at myself in the mirror and feel anything but shame for making this deal when I know I am innocent?"

I was innocent and there was no way in the world I would admit to guilt, certainly not as a matter of convenience. I could have had the opportunity to spend very little time in jail, but I would have to live with the label of convicted rapist for the rest of my life, and that was something I wasn't willing to do, not for anything in the world. Choices have consequences, and I wasn't willing to choose the easy way out if it meant changing who I was.

A short while later I was taken into the courtroom. The jury had reached its verdict. My hands were sweating and I felt like I was going to puke. I could barely think. Please get it right, please get it right, I said to myself. Not guilt. Not guilty. Not guilty, I mumbled. When everyone was inside, the jury foreman stood. I sat up straight and proud, in my black suit and starched white shirt. It felt like an eternity for the words to come out of his mouth. I kept telling myself, "it's going to be okay, James. It's going to be okay, James." A bad feeling crept over me as I scanned the looks on their faces. I tried to remain calm, but it felt like my heart was going to burst out of my chest. The clerk asked me to stand up. My throat tightened. I slowly pushed back my chair, my hands shaking in fear. I took a breath, regained my composure and stood firmly.

The clerk asked the Foreman for the verdict.

On the first count of kidnapping: Guilty.

On the count of sexual assault: Guilty.

On the count of robbery: Guilty.

On the count of assault: Guilty.

On the count of larceny: Guilty.

"No!" I could hear my mother's cries behind me as the courtroom became a blur of activity and noise. I stood in shock. The price for my innocence and integrity: I was now officially a convicted rapist.

At that moment, the power to convict was clearly stronger than my own convictions.

Chapter 8

TESTING MY CODE

The TV show view of prison is that you drive up to this building surrounded by barbed wire and then your life goes through some kind of change as you go from the outside world into this new prison-world. That's not what it's like for prisoners. I was shackled and chained and shoved into the back of a van that looked like an ice cream truck. I sat on a bench near the front, so I could barely see out the sliver of a window in the back to see my freedom trailing away as we were driven to Somers prison. While how someone carries him or herself says a lot, I believe there are times when you can look at someone and see their spirit. I didn't go into prison a rapist or even a violent person, though I was flawed and had been violent at times. But to see my spirit on that day as I sat on that bench was to see pure hatred. I took all of the anger about my wrongful conviction and I carried it inside of me. I hated the judge. I hated the jury. I hated the victim. I hated the lawyers–I hated everyone and I let that hate consume me. I think a lot of us do this at times—we take our feelings about someone else—the boss that fired us, the spouse that left us, the friend that treated us badly, and we put our feelings on them, and then inside of us. So we at once hate someone else, and become the hate, and in my case, it was pretty intense. I was becoming the monster I needed to be to survive.

Almost instantly, the rules changed. It didn't matter what or who I was on the outside, but how I carried myself inside prison. The code that served me well on the outside—to carry myself with the courage of my convictions, to never stop believing in myself—was now my means of survival. The prison code dictated that as a convicted rapist, I would become a target. My code said that if you're coming at me, you better bring your best, because if you're taking me out, I will take you down with me if I have to. The only thing that mattered now was keeping my sanity and not getting killed.

I didn't even know we were in the prison until the van stopped, and while I didn't get that TV-version experience, I knew just sitting there that I was in a bad place—I could feel it in the intensity of everyone around me. The guards came to the door and we were led out like cattle into a room known as "The Bullpen," a place where prisoners are transitioned, either coming in, or on their way out to court or another prison. It was strangely quiet, like guys were walking to a funeral, saving up their energy for when they needed to show it most, in front of other prisoners. The room was unremarkable, it looked like an empty office room, except that it was occupied by a bunch of prisoners. The feeling in the room, however, was totally remarkable. Anytime you put ten prisoners in a room there will be tension, but put ten new prisoners in a room? Man, watch out. In this case, there were nine African Americans and one Caucasian. When I walked into these doors, I was James Tillman, convicted rapist, but the men in the Bullpen heard about my trial, the deal I rejected and my claims of innocence. Even if they didn't think I was innocent, they knew that they heard me talk about how unfair I thought the process was. They were angry for me, and they wanted to take action. The guys started to whisper to each other, and finally one of them turned to me and said, "James, do you want to take him down?" nodding his head towards the White guy. "They screwed you, man. Let's mess him up." I could see the terror in the White man's eyes. Whatever he was outside of prison–he could have been the toughest guy in his neighborhood–here he was in a room filled with eight people ready to take him out. Standing near him, I could feel the tension in his body, see the sweat forming on his head. He stared at me, not saying a word, not taking his eyes off me. Without talking he was pleading for his life. It was as if he was saying, 'c'mon man, it wasn't me. I'm a prisoner, too.' I looked at him, and then the other guys. I could feel the rage building in the Bullpen. We were all angry about finding ourselves here, waiting for our descent into life's version of hell. It was enough to make you want to explode. I got the vibe. Hell, I was probably angrier than any of them. Would this be my chance to send a message saying, 'don't mess with James Tillman?' I looked at the White guy again, and realized that the code I developed had a new element: that we are defined by the choices we make. That became crystal clear to me during the trial, as I chose to reject the deal, so the choices I made in prison started to make more sense to me. More than wanting to prove how tough I was, I was determined to prove that I would make the right choice whenever I could. I knew what it was like to be judged, so I didn't want to judge this guy. I also wanted to reinforce my own survival code: leave me alone, and I'll leave you alone. I turned to the guy and said, "no, no man. I'm good." I could feel the White guy's sense of relief. I wasn't a hero or anything. In fact, I knew nothing about this man–he could have been a murderer for all I knew, but I held strongly to the values of justice and fairness. If we attacked that guy, I would be like all the people who sent me to prison. Taking that guy down, as much as it might have helped me release some of the hatred I felt, just would have been the wrong thing to do. I just got sentenced to prison for a crime I didn't commit. I wasn't going to let myself meet that injustice with another one–this one on my hands.

Soon we were paraded through a familiar process. We were taken to a room where I had to give up my navy blue suit. I looked so good in that suit–like one of the lawyers. I traded that in for a pair of prison browns. Holding my clothes and wearing only underwear, I was taken to a room where they sprayed me with delousing powder. Next I was led to the shower, and then I changed into my drab tan uniform–my transformation from James Tillman, Free Man, to Prisoner was now complete. With every step I took into my new prison life, it was getting harder and harder to believe in anything, to have faith, or hope that any good could come out of this experience.

Chapter 9

THE FIRST DAY

Your first kiss. Your first date. The birth of your first child. The first day of work at your first job. Your child's first steps. Life is full of "firsts," positive experiences that become pivotal moments in our lives.

My imprisonment meant that I missed out on many of those "firsts." In prison, my firsts came in different forms. The first day in a new prison. The first day with a new cell mate–or "cellie" as they were called. The first day in solitary confinement. And the first time you experience something unbelievably horrible, even by prison standards. It happened on the first day of my incarceration after I was wrongfully convicted.

I was led down the cold confines of a narrow hall. Drab concrete blocks, draped like curtains, hung all around me. As I rounded the corner, the guard barked at me to walk straight ahead. With each step into this new world, my mind raced, but I refused to show any emotion. I was taking it all in. I was walking so fast, I didn't have time to absorb my surroundings. I was on-guard, tense, focused on carrying myself to send the right message: don't mess with me, and I was kind of looking at everything, but looking at nothing at the same time; seeing the world around me, but not making eye contact with anyone or anything.

I turned another corner and felt a strange feeling. Do you know how sometimes your mind and body can use intuition to process things even before you even understand them? You react to sensations before you even know what's going on. That's what was happening to me, and with every step I took, I felt like I was coming out of a fog. What I was seeing slowly came in to focus, like someone was playing with the zoom lens on a camera. I realized something really bad was happening. My stomach was turning. With each step, things became more clear, until finally I recognized this "thing," and at once a tidal wave of adrenaline raced through my body.

Snapping to attention, I froze for a moment to take it in, and then it hit me—what I was looking at wasn't so unbelievable—it was horribly real. Sprinting towards it, the world around me seemed still and indifferent—motionless.

"Oh my God! What do I do? What do I do?" I screamed at myself, panicking. My heart racing, my palms sweating, I couldn't think—I just went into action. I put my arms around this awkwardly large lump, but I couldn't undo the contraption. I struggled to lift it, to no avail. I did everything I could to relieve the tension, but nothing worked—it was too much for me. I stood there, locked in an unholy embrace, frantic. "Hey, someone, help me!" I yelled. Nothing. No response.

I felt a twitch and then a kick. Slipping through my arms, I hugged as hard as I could and lifted with everything I had. Still nothing. The tension eased a little but it was too much for me to handle alone.

"Hey, someone help me," I screamed, letting go and running down the hall. I finally spotted two Hispanic guys hanging out nearby. I ran up to them, breathless but determined, "come on, you've got to help me." The site of me barking orders at them probably left them confused, but to their credit they bolted out of their trance and followed me down the hall. "On three. One, two, three." I wrapped my arms around the bottom while the other two guys lifted from the top. Then as quickly as they helped me, they were gone.

There it lay on the ground, this thing I struggled with–this man, a person, a soul–who tried to take his own life. He lay there next to me, blood surging back into his body, while I sat next to him panting, sweat running down my forehead, trying to catch my breath. No words were spoken, but if I could hear him in that moment, had I spent more time in prison, I'm certain he would have said to me, 'why didn't you let me die?'

Chapter 10

LIFE IN PRISON

I was led out of the cell and back down the hall in silence. I just saved a man's life and there was scant proof of it–almost like it was an inconvenience–a light bulb in the hallway that popped and needed to be changed. The conviction I felt in that life-affirming moment was a sign of my will to persevere, and a statement about how cruelly indifferent my new surroundings were. A will to survive waging war against a culture breeding inhumanity, that in some ways tries to kill parts of you. This war would be waged for the course of my 18½ years in prison.

Somers was crowded, so an area that formerly housed ping pong and pool tables was converted into a "dorm." When you walk into "the block," the Corrections Officer, or CO, greets you. The CO in charge of this area holds enormous power over you. My first CO was a 60-year old white guy, who for reasons I don't understand, gave me a coveted job as a "Tier Man," which involved cleaning the place and handing out things like toilet paper. When I got that job, I was determined to be so good at it that I'd never lose it.

Bunk beds were stacked like dominoes, one next to the other, filling the room, which was enclosed with thick glass walls. It was like living in a giant fishbowl. The showers and bathrooms were adjacent to the room, so except for going to rec or to get food, I pretty much lived in this space 24x7. It felt like a dark, desolate cave within a cave, only mine had glass walls. This was my new home.

After a short while in the dorm, I was moved to B Block. The blocks were like self-contained prisons within the prison. Walk into the block and you're greeted by the CO and the guard's desk. Then ahead of you were two large squares, one sitting on top of the other, each precisely divided by two intersecting hallways, dividing the block into four squares with each holding about 25 cells. When in B Block, I moved into a cell for the first time, and still kept my job as Tier Man. But as much as I liked my new space, the one constant about prison life is that there is no constant. Things are always changing. I not only jumped around from cell to cell, I served time in pretty much every prison in the state.

My time in prison was an unimaginable hell, and I don't choose those words lightly. I say unimaginable, because it is so hard for those of you reading this to imagine what prison life is really like, even if you watch one of those reality shows on television. I remember seeing a documentary on TV when I was younger called Scared Straight, where prisoners talked to kids to give them a realistic look at prison life. You can watch that and get a glimpse of what life is like for those of us inside, but at some point you turn off your TV, you go back to your life and you don't appreciate how relentless it is behind bars. Relentless boredom. Relentless fear. Relentless violence. It never ends.

When most people recall events, they think about them in a linear fashion, driven by the facts. Anyone who sits in history class can remember that first one thing happened, and then the next thing logically happened, and then there was a predictable end result. History, tied up in a nice, neat package. Those who have experienced traumatic events will tell you that it works almost the opposite way for us. I can tell you about the major events, and I can recall in more detail than I would like some of the most horrific things that can be experienced by a person. But to present it all in some nice linear timeline makes no sense to me, because that's not how I experienced my sentence. Yes, time marched on from the first to the last day of my incarceration, but it was driven more by feelings about events–that's how I distinguished one day from the next. 'Oh, that was the day I saw that nasty fight,' or 'that was the day my mom visited and smiled a lot.' That's how I experienced time because to sit and think about 45 years ticking off minute by minute, day by day, would drive me nuts. What is 45 years? It's hard to get your head around just how long that is. When you spend day after day after day after day after day in the same place, going through the same routine, the thought of time on a daily or weekly basis becomes confused, everything just blurs together. I was known for the time I was spending in prison. My days were marked by time, and the sense of time drove everything we did, but the concept of time was also lost on me. I didn't care about it anymore. That was the irony of my relationship to time. Monday. Tuesday. Wednesday. Thursday. Friday. Saturday. Sunday. Days blended into weeks. Weeks became months. Months turned into years. Holidays. Birthdays. Anniversaries. 4th of July. Columbus Day. Veterans Day. Spring. Summer. Fall. Winter. All of these things defined by time, yet none of it mattered to me, because of the time that was taken away from me.

That's how I remember my prison life. I was picked out of my world, and put in this totally foreign world, and my sense of time just vanished. Poof. Gone. So I hope you offer me some forgiveness if I don't give you a linear account of my days in prison–what happened from one day to the next, one year to the next, because the God's honest truth is, I don't want to remember. In fact, I've spent most of my time since leaving prison trying to forget.

I think the best way I can explain what prison life is like is to compare it to the kind of typical life on the outside. So consider this: you're about 35, married, the proud parent of two children, living in a house in the suburbs. You're lying in your comfortable King Bed, with the extra blankets. You reach over, sleepily turn off the alarm and hit snooze to catch a few more minutes of rest, and curl up next to your wife in the warmth of your bed. Your arm rests gently on her as you pull her close.

You're lying in your darkened cell. The smell of rancid bowel movements lingers. You lie there on the flimsy mattress in a cold, small twin bed that barely fits your oversized frame. You shoot out of bed, knowing you need to wake up early and get ready. Morning is the most dangerous time. You had a terrible night's sleep. Another night filled with nightmares and bad dreams. Dreams so dark and horrible, scenes of violence, murder and suicide haunt you, but you can't let that show. You shove the feelings inside. Another night of noises, smells and artificial lights. You've got to get up. You don't have the luxury of time. Not now. You have to get going.

Back home in the suburbs, you kiss your wife as she falls back to sleep. Your feet hit the smoothly polished floor as you walk to your private bathroom. As you gain your senses, your mind begins to wander. You think about your day at work, or maybe seeing your child in a school play later that day. You reach into your medicine cabinet, replace your worn-out razor blade and shave. You admire your work as you rinse your face, staring at yourself in the mirror and following the lines on your face, wondering how time has left its measure. You sit on the toilet in the privacy of your own room and pick up a magazine. Then it's off to the shower, where you stand alone and ease your way into the day.

In the cell, you walk a few steps to the stainless steel toilet which is filled with the rancid smells from the night before. No privacy, just a toilet and a sink right smack in the room. Your cellie snores loudly as you sit on the fully exposed toilet. From there, you turn to the sink, brush your teeth with the worn-out toothbrush and shave with the dull razor that you've labored with for weeks on end. You're not getting a new razor because you can't afford it, or because it's a security risk. There's no shower. No morning paper. Not even breakfast. Nothing. Just you and your cellie in a small, suffocating concrete and steel cell. You know that morning is the most unpredictably violent time in prison, so you ready yourself. When the doors pop open and a mass of people are driven to one place or another like cattle, attacks usually occur, with weapons refined in the dark of night and plans executed with great care and precision. If you want a chance at a hot meal and a decent breakfast, you have to be one of the first out of your cell and in the food line. However, as one of the first out the door, alone in the halls, more opportunities are present for you to be jumped. The safest place in any line is in the back. You walk the halls on guard, literally doing your best to watch your back, keeping it against the wall. You sit at breakfast with your back to the wall, the room open in front of you. You always have everyone in front of you so that you can keep an eye on things. Knowing this, you begin your own daily regimen to prepare yourself for the moment the doors open.

At home, you get out of the shower and go to your large closet to pick out today's outfit, not giving a thought to who might be around the next corner waiting for you. You think about hitting the treadmill at they gym to get some exercise, but decide to do that later on your way home. You have that luxury to plan your day and be spontaneous.

Back in prison, you put on your standard top and pants. I walked into prison in a black suit. It was elegant. My mother bought it for me for the trial. I remember walking into prison thinking about the irony–

here I was, probably looking my best, like the CEO of a company. A few minutes later I was stripped of all my clothing, naked and undergoing a humiliating physical inspection. And then I put on tan slacks and a tan tee shirt–my prison uniform. Colors I would grow to hate with every fiber of my being. Day after day, the same clothes. No choices. Just a tan shirt and pants. After dressing, to prepare yourself mentally and physically for the day ahead, you hit the floor, face down. You fix one hand firmly on the ground, and then position the other. You can almost taste the smell of the concrete floor as it lays below you. Your feet perched out, your back stiff as a board, your abs tucked in tight, you press your body up. Then down. Up. Then down. Faster and faster. Counting the repetitions in your head. Ten by ten. Then fifty by fifty. Eventually you end up in the hundreds. Push up after push up. Sit up after sit up. Dip after dip. The sweat pouring, your heart pounding. Calling on the limitless well of rage and anger, you're working, straining, literally pushing your body to the absolute physical limit. As 6 a.m. nears, your muscles bulging, you stand ready to face the day, and beat the living hell out of it if necessary. It's kill or be killed. That's the mentality. Every minute of every day.

Back at home, you walk downstairs, pet the dog, open the front door, take a deep breath and take in the first wiff of the morning air. The smell of grass lingers on the warm breeze. You bend down and get your morning paper. You walk to the pantry and then open the fridge. 'Should I have cereal or eggs,' you wonder? You look at the choices. Fresh fruit. Pancakes and Vermont Maple Syrup. You settle for oatmeal and orange juice–fresh squeezed, no pulp. So many options. You flip through the morning paper. There are stories about politicians and political posturing, petty crimes and kids in trouble with drugs (maybe some are being sent to prison). Choosing to ignore the bad news, you sit and read the sports section and listen to the weather on television. After breakfast you scribble a note to your wife to wish her a good day and you hop in your car for the drive to work. You pull out your phone and plug it in, enjoying a few last minutes of peace before you arrive at your building. When you arrive, you pull into a parking space and make your way to the office. As you pass the security guard you make polite conversation about the basketball game on TV last night. On the way to your office you pass a friend who gently ribs you about the outfit you're wearing. Then a friend yells out to ask how your daughter's soccer game went last night. Then a colleague walks over to you, wishes you good morning and reminds you that a meeting is about to start in the conference room. With that, you walk to the door, open it, warmly shake hands and begin your day.

In prison, the doors are about to open. They never open at exactly the same time, so you stand near the door, anxiously waiting, but never, ever, letting it show. You think back to the day you were first brought to prison. Shackled and chained, you were put in a caged bus–a cage within a cage–and driven beyond the gates, the barbed wire and the guards, leaving the green grass behind forever. It was the one commute you wished would take longer than expected. If you were lucky, you might even hit traffic. When the doors opened, a mass of humanity was on the block. Prisoners, like animals, are caged in sections and released in blocks. You make your way through the block and you are greeted by the other prisoners with words so foul they would incite a riot on the outside of prison, but here, it's just normal talk.

If you're one of the first to arrive at breakfast, the food is passable, and then you can use your breakfast to barter for something better. But for the most part, breakfast is horrible. Lunch is horrible. Dinner is horrible. It's hard to see how the food passes as acceptable. You certainly wouldn't choose to feed any of it to your family on the outside. But you have no choice. You eat it. You find a way to hold your breath as you eat, and just take the food down for its nutritional value. On a good day, it doesn't give you the runs. On most days, you're going to the commissary to buy food, using the money you earn in prison by working. If you're lucky and you get to lunch early and you have hot food, you can take it to someone you know who likes it, and offer a trade, curry some favor. Maybe some French toast for fries at dinner. Maybe the food buys you some protection. Maybe it's an offer of goodwill to be used later. Everything, and I mean everything, in prison is used as a means for survival. I don't know much, but I do know that food has always been the way to a man's heart, and that was certainly the case in prison.

At work, a friend surprises you with a visit. You hang out for a bit, talking about the game of golf you played last week or the movie you saw over the weekend. The visit is casual and organic. Maybe it only lasts a few minutes, but you don't have to worry about planning anything because you're confident you'll see each other soon.

In prison, the CO gives you a pass to go to the visiting room. If you're in your cell, he hands it to you, or more likely, you get called to his desk and you wait for a convenient time for him to give it to you. If he has something going on or you've done something wrong, you may not get it. Before you leave, you run back to your cell and spray yourself with deodorant or air freshener—prisons stink, and you don't want your visitor to be offended. You walk to the visiting room and it's the only time that you get a feel for how big this place really is. With all the checkpoints along the way, it feels like it takes an eternity to get there. If you have visits that allow contact, you walk into a room that looks like the food court at the mall, with guards standing everywhere. The visitors coming in most likely got a shake down—a frisk—before they got to the table. If there was trouble that day, the guards might make everyone's life difficult. If you are lucky, you might be able to have a private conversation. Some crooked lawyers would smuggle contraband in when they could, not because they wanted the money, but because they hated the system and wanted to mess with the guards. When I had a visitor, it was one of two people: my mother or my little brother, Dennis. It was always good to see them, but it was always brief.

At work, your meet your wife for lunch. You sit at an outdoor table at a popular café. You enjoy a nice lunch and order dessert, but then you think about the steak you'll be having for dinner tonight—you are watching your calories after all—so you take just one bite and leave the rest. The waiter takes your plate to the kitchen and throws the food you didn't eat in the trash. After work, you hit the gym on the way home. The personal trainer you hired to get you back in shape yells at you to motivate you, and then shakes your hand and slaps you on the back as you walk out the door. At home, you enjoy a nice dinner with your wife. After dinner, you chat with your neighbors, send some emails on your computer, and then you and your wife watch television together, flipping through one of a hundred channels before gently falling asleep in each other's arms.

Back in prison, you move when you are told to move. You go to your cell when you're told to go to your cell. If the air conditioning or heat is working, it's a good day. If you get a chance to have rec—outdoor time—you go just to smell the outdoors for a few minutes. If there's any yelling or screaming, it's because someone wants to cut you or kill you. If you have a chance to sit with a visitor, you sit behind impenetrable glass, sometimes without any contact. In addition to your morning workout, you'll workout at lunch and in the evening. You work when you're told to work, where you're told to work. You are treated like a dog by some of the guards who are cursing you, putting you down. Gangs might be coming after you. Someone might look at you wrong or insult you, and then you'd be in a nasty fight. You might get beaten and put in solitary confinement, lose rec or TV time. At some point, after a long draining day, you crawl back into that tiny bed with the flimsy mattress, and you hear the door roll and slam shut. Locked in, no way out, you sit and stare. One more day done. Thousands more to go.

That's what it was like for me, day after day, after day, after day… and with each passing day, I became more lost, more broken. I wasn't only confined to life in prison, I became engulfed in a prison of my own making–one of hopelessness and despair, one where I couldn't find a way to believe in anything. I was starting to lose faith.

Chapter 11

PASSING TIME:
PUBLIC TV, MUFANGO & REC

I held the envelope as if I didn't know its contents. My stomach churned with anticipation. I imagine this is what it might feel like being a nominee at one of those big awards shows in Hollywood, or for kids holding a college acceptance letter. I coveted the moment, and I didn't want to share it with anyone. I got back to my cell, where I could sit in private, and stared at the unremarkable white envelope. Its contents held my judgment. Incredibly, I knew the result, I knew exactly what was inside that letter, but still, I held some faint glimmer of hope that maybe, this one time, it might be different.

I calmly tore open the envelope, and flattened out the piece of paper, pausing before reading it. I held it up, bringing it closer to my eyes.

The verdict...2034.

No change in my status. I turned my head away from the paper in disappointment. "Damn," I said, looking at the piece of paper that summarized my time served in prison. I ripped up the paper and threw it out, and then sat back on my bed. Another long day facing me. Another sleepless night. Another wary morning. Another day in this horrible place.

2034 seemed like an eternity to me. I couldn't even imagine what life would be like when I got out. Would anyone I know still be alive? Where will I live? What will my house be like? What will cars look like? I'd be 73 years when I got out. Could I get a job? How would I get by if most of my friends and family are dead or don't care about me anymore?

I was moved around a lot. I spent time in every major prison in Connecticut. I spent most of my time at first in Somers, then later at Cheshire. I also spent time in the SuperMax facility at Northern in Somers, which was like living in a dungeon. The walls were gray and concrete. There was almost no color in that place, and being a SuperMax, the windows were tiny–like slivers–they were about four inches wide and a foot high. At one point, I was moved to Virginia for a year as part of a prisoner sharing program to bring relief to prison overcrowding. Prison is awful everywhere, but Virginia was nasty, just really dangerous and violent. I was grateful to be moved back to Connecticut when the opportunity presented itself. Cheshire, which was opened in 1909, felt every bit of its age. Cheshire was overcrowded and for a good stretch of time–over a month–the air conditioning didn't work. But as long as we didn't die, nobody really cared. The conditions were almost unbearable. During the time I spent in prison, the prison population almost quadrupled, from roughly 5,000 to nearly 20,000 inmates. I didn't know the exact figure until I got out, but I could tell at the time that something was going on, because the place was bursting at the seams. I wasn't sure what was happening outside–police getting tougher, laws changing, more bad people being produced, but inside it was getting awfully crowded.

Rec was our recess, and if there were only 50 kids from a grade at school recess there wouldn't be a problem in our rec area, but in my case there were usually around 400-500 angry men cramped into a tight space. That's a recipe for disaster, and it's where a lot of trouble started. So, I would usually just stick close to my workout partner, do my thing, and get out of there.

I spent a lot of time in prison in my cell, sometimes as much as 23 hours a day. If I was lucky, I had a tiny window, a 13-inch TV, a walkman cassette radio, a toilet and maybe something to read. For nights when I couldn't sleep, I'd take Benadryl–anything to get me through a night.

I did consider myself a Christian those early days in prison, but it's hard to walk with Christ when you're filled with hate, so in reality I was a Christian in name only. I struggled mightily with my faith. I sat alone in my cell and cursed God more than I praised Him. I couldn't understand how an all-loving God could do this to me when He knew I was innocent. Why am I locked up? I walked away from my faith. I eventually gave up on God and Christianity. I explored other faiths through the years, but nothing rang true to me because the hate and anger were always most present. Hate and anger are like masks that possess you and prevent you from believing in anything other than how strongly you hate. I couldn't possibly feel love for the Lord when I was so consumed with hate.

Over the course of my tenure, I had a lot of different cellies. The configuration of the space never really changed, so the roommate really made it a good or bad experience. If you were lucky, you had a guy who was quiet, clean and respectful–someone who washed his hands after going to the bathroom and who used deodorant. Most of the cellies snored loud, so I went to bed most nights wearing headphones. One of my favorite cellies was a talented singer, he made time pass nicely.

This is going to sound very strange coming from a prison inmate, but public television was one of my favorite ways to pass time and something I really looked forward to. I never had the opportunity to travel, so I used to sit in my cell and watch shows about all these exotic places. Then after I watched the show, I would lay on my cot, close my eyes and imagine myself walking on a beach in a warm tropical climate, the waves gently crashing in rhythm. Swoosh. Swoosh. Swoosh. I'd imagine the warm breeze gently flowing around, and feel the sun beat against my body. This was my vacation. I really looked forward to these moments where I could dream of walking on a remote sandy beach, or I might pretend to visit the Coliseum in Rome or a castle in France. I loved the time spent alone watching public TV in my cell, nobody bothering me. Just me, lost in a world so far away from the reality of life in prison.

Because the food in prison was awful, we had to get creative to get by. There is no polite way around this: the food sucked. You always wanted to hurry to breakfast to be one of the first so that you had a chance of eating hot food, or, more important, so that you could use your hot food to bargain with someone else for something you might want or need. It seemed we were always waiting in line. We ate by blocks of prisoners, so one block would be eating and then another one would move in. There were usually about 100 guys either waiting in line or eating. Breakfast was around 6 am and it consisted of a donut, egg product, white bread and farina.

Since I love food so much, I also loved experimenting with food. We made concoctions out of whatever we could in prison. One of my favorite things to do to pass time, and to get some decent food, was to make something I concocted out of stuff bought at the Commissary. Through work, I was able to earn a modest amount of money, which most of us used to buy things at the Commissary, rather than having to eat every meal at the cafeteria. Using leftovers or things we bought at the Commissary, I was able to make Mafungo and The Thing.

To make Mafungo you need hot water, potato chips, Slim Jims and some bean dip and sausages. You take the sausages and Slim Jims and cut them into small pieces. If you happen to have fish that day, you can replace the sausage with fish. Take out the potato chips and put the bean dip in the bag, then run hot water over it to heat it up. Next put the Slim Jims and sausage in the bag. Then you add the chips back in and either use the chips as a dip or eat the whole thing smashed together. You won't find that recipe on the Food Channel, but it was awesome!

A friend of mine invented "The Thing" in the SuperMax prison, where we didn't have access to a lot of the essentials. For The Thing, you also need a bag of potato chips, Slim Jims, rice and soup (that you'd take from lunch or dinner). First you take the skin off the Slim Jims and break off little pieces. Then you take the bag of potato chips and crush the chips, adding in the soup and rice. Next you take the potato chip bag and keep running hot water over it. Eventually, the contents of the bag heat up, but it always took a while. It's not worthy of a cooking show, but locked in a SuperMax cell it was gourmet food to me.

On weekends, we would get visits from Alpha Ministries, who would take Christian prisoners to a room and spend the entire day in worship and retreat. For many years, I chose to stay away from these programs, but after I while, I decided to sign up if for no other reason than it was a good way to pass time. Later, however, I grew to value these experiences almost more than anything else, and I would go just to be with people who also loved The Lord—they were like family to me.

I also signed up to spend time in the law library. If you were lucky, you might get help from someone—a well-read inmate, but more often than not those inmates were transferred a lot, so you were really on your own in there. I spent time in the library trying to research and learn more about my case and my legal options. I also wanted to keep up with my reading, which I had to work hard to do. I didn't feel like I had an attorney that I could trust—in fact I didn't feel like I could trust anyone—so I had to educate myself to get a basic understanding of the law.

The prison clothes grew to be monotonous. We were given three pairs of the tan outfit—that was my wardrobe. After several years in prison, the state made a slight change to the tan outfit, giving us a dark brown shirt. To me, it felt like I was wearing a tuxedo. It felt so good to wear something different. While it was just a tee shirt, I felt like I hit the lottery! We had our clothes laundered once a week, which is great if you're living on the outside and you have a nice closet full of clothes, but in prison, it's hard to stretch that out sometimes. So guys really tend to stink. One of the more surprising things for people coming into prison is the smell, the unique smell of thousands of men jammed into a confined space. If you lose your sense of sight in prison because you don't see the outside and everything always looks the same: same dull colors, same physical shapes—your sense of smell is certainly heightened, or at least mine was. But guys got around this by washing a lot of their little clothes in the shower, like underwear, socks, shorts, tee shirts. At one point, the Commissary started to sell scented oils. I'd borrow a hat from a kitchen worker and rub the oil in the hat and then put it on my fan, which made the cell smell so much better. Consider it creative air freshening!

Doing laundry in the shower might make the prison smell nicer, and guys feel cleaner, but it took up valuable shower time. We had an hour to shower, shave and make calls. That sounds like a lot of time, but we had roughly 100 guys for six showers. And if everyone's doing laundry in the shower, things got real tight. The bottom line is that I had a few minutes of shower time each day, and so one of the biggest physical feats of the day was the race to the shower. Getting to the showers quickly was like summiting Everest every day, and man it felt good to reach the summit first.

Rehabilitation classes were one of the most positive aspects of prison life. They gave me hope, allowed me to prepare for a life outside prison, and kept me constructively engaged in something positive. Through these classes, I could actually take college courses in prison, which I loved. I took the History of Western Civilization—Western Civ 1 as we called it—from a white woman who was a part-time college professor. I remember during the entire course just being skeptical. Although I had a hard time trusting white women at that point in my life, there was something about her that began to break me down a little. The best way to describe me in that class was distant and difficult, but she didn't give up on me. I signed up for Western Civ 2 when the course was complete, again, primarily to pass the time, but deep down also to continue my connection to this teacher. One day after class, she asked if she could talk to me.

"James, I'm having trouble reaching you. Do you want to talk?" she asked. She opened the door, and I intuitively walked in. I told her my story, explaining my innocence. I noticed her body posture change as I talked with her, and I felt mine change too. I loosened up, became less tense. As I explained my circumstances, she began to cry. When I was done, she said words that would put one of the first cracks in my steel resolve: "I'm sorry," she said to me, looking me straight in the eyes. She was one of the first people who I felt genuinely listened to me. I don't know if she believed me, but she heard me, and that meant so much to me.

I sat in my cell that night, thinking about that experience. I learned so much that day, not just about Western Civilization, but about life. I realized that I can't stereotype anyone—hate this person just because she was white and a woman. That experience helped solidify one of the central elements of my code, one that drives me to this day: don't judge anyone by a label.

I developed a genuine respect and admiration for my teacher, and something else remarkable happened as well. I began to excel in class, and I really started to learn a lot. Unfortunately, in a political move that was popular with the public, the Governor at the time stopped the rehabilitation program, ending these educational opportunities. It broke my heart.

One of the worst places to pass time in prison is in Medical–what most people think of as the sick ward. Nobody wants to be sick or injured, but if you have to be sick with anything, prison is the absolute last place you want to be. If you don't feel well, you have to tell your CO. If the guard feels like your sickness is life threatening or needs urgent attention, they will act immediately. If they feel it's anything but an emergency, the guards make you fill out a request form. Yeah, it sounds crazy, but you have to ask to be sick. If the request is approved, they take you to medical. But if they don't, and I think they have a different definition of what it means to be sick than most medical professionals do outside of prison, they make you wait. A lot of times, when I had the flu for example, I had to go to the Commissary to buy my own pills and just wait it out.

If you're on the prison medical staff, chances are you're not the stereotypical affluent physician in private practice. Put another way, those providing medical care aren't exactly on the list of the Top 100 physicians in the state.

Near the end of my time in prison, I was out playing basketball. I loved playing ball. On this particular day, someone passed me the ball. I confidently grabbed it, bent my knees, went up for the shot, released the ball and came back down. The second I left the ground I felt a snap in my ankle and heard a loud "pop." As I landed, I fell to the ground in agonizing pain. My Achilles tendon popped, and it was very serious.

I was taken to Medical on an emergency basis. Once the nature of my injury was determined, I was scheduled to have my tendon repaired. I was taken to a hospital for the repair job, but the surgery was so bad that I needed a second operation to repair the repair job. To this day, I am still grappling with intense pain and at times I walk with a limp. The only reason I am suffering this badly is because I was in prison. Had I not been in prison and was able to receive the same kind of care everyone else has outside of prison, I am sure my operation would have gone better. My time in prison literally compromised my health.

One of the questions I'm asked most often is about the guards: what they were really like and how they treated me. Through TV shows and movies, there is definitely a perception built around prison guards. What I found with the guards is basically true of most people: there are people who make good choices and bad choices. The choices people make sometimes lead to a corruption of the spirit, or an enlightening of the spirit. There were guards that seemed to bring their problems to work and take all of life's frustrations out on us—and there were others who genuinely wanted to use the experience to turn us around. These guards were professional—they didn't cross any lines by using excessive force or verbally abusing us. Rather, they would talk to us, get to know us as people, maybe talk about the importance of religion or hard work. They were there not just to provide security, but they realized that the best way to keep things safe and sane was to treat the inmates as humans – the ones who also treated the guards with respect. All guards followed the same rules, and the rules were very clear: do what they say, when they say it, but the rules were certainly enforced differently. So it was always worth it to me to take time to get the know the guards so that I could better understand how the rules were going to be enforced. I realized that I didn't need to look for trouble in prison. Because of the way guards work, you never really get to know someone for very long. Most guards are rotated every 4–6 months. The prison bosses moved people around quite a bit. There is a CO in charge of each block and that person essentially reports to the warden, who may as well have been the President of the United States to me— someone that has great power, is seen and heard, but distant and not really experienced.

There was one guard who I really admired. Of course he enforced the rules, but he had a sense of humanity, and he was wickedly funny; he was like a stand-up comic. He loved to tease me. I guess it was his way of taking the tension out of the situation, and I respected him for that.

Despite all the things I did to pass time in prison, nothing brought me any measure of lasting peace. The Mufango and The Thing were good, but eventually I'd get hungry again, thinking of that steak dinner I missed so long ago. I'd go anywhere my imagination would take me, but it would never last. The television always went off. The dreams always faded. I'd sit there, alone in my cell, surrounded by angry prisoners, concrete walls and steel bars, all shouting their indifference to me. I was alone in this world, but never really alone.

Chapter 12

MY PRISON OF HATE

My body tense, standing in my cell, the cold concrete beneath my feet, my hands wrapped around thick steel bars. A sterile concrete wall a few feet to my right, another a few feet to my left. The toilet, cot and sink behind me, a dark and dirty concrete ceiling braced just above my head. Stuffed inside the tight confines of a cold dark box, no place to move physically, and no place to escape my feelings. The things that went through my mind are so dark that I can't even write them here, but to look at my face, to see my eyes, you could see it, feel it.

What was once a world full of colors and natural smells was now monotone and monochrome. I put on the tan uniform and blended into the unremarkably redundant surroundings. I didn't realize at the time just how much I'd grow to hate the color brown–18 years of the same uniforms. You don't realize what you take for granted until it's all taken away from you, even the right to pick your own clothes. The light was artificial. The smells were artificial. The place was loud, like a constant babble. Nothing was real, yet it was horribly real, every bit of it.

I was full of hate going into prison. I hated the system. I hated the guards. I hated the inmates. I hated the judge. I hated the jury. I hated the victim. I hated everyone…except my family. I carried that anger with me. Hate and injustice fueled me. It's what got me through a day. I needed to hate to survive, crazy as that sounds. But prison is, in essence, about a unique brand of hate. To some, the opposite of love is hate, but the truth is, the opposite of love is nothing – just not caring. It wasn't that I hated everything as much as I just didn't care about anything or anyone anymore.

The truth is I lived life on the other side of hate, in the shadows of humanity. Where some people dwell in moments of their lives, I now lived openly. The place where most people fear to go—that was my home, not for hours or days, but for weeks, months and years. To simply hate, that means you're still engaged in the process of life, but to not care…it wasn't like I lived in darkness, but rather I became the darkness. This is precisely why it took so long to write this book. Who in their right mind wants to connect back to this world?

The longer I spent in prison, the more I really started to struggle. Living with the hate was worse than being convicted. The sentence was a judgment, but the hate became a way of life. I regret the hate I held and lived with more than the prison sentence itself, as strange as that may sound.

But here's the key to the whole thing: I wasn't alone in feeling the anger or hatred. Almost everyone in prison felt the same way. It's hard in prison to find any reason to hope, or anything to feel good about. We all just sat there in a cesspool of our unique brand of hate and indifference.

Most of us think of hatred and we think about that one moment in time, when we got robbed or cut off in the car, when someone said something that hurt us, but for me, hatred was time. I moved with hate. I slept with hate. I ate with hate. I carried that hate to the point where you couldn't distinguish where it started and I began. That was my view of my world, and that's what it was like inside me if you could see into my soul. Every moment I spent in prison was a reminder of my innocence, and it ignited in me a deep well of hatred. For some guys who earned their convictions, the days were ticked off against their sentence. For me, each moment, each day, was another day lost while I sat innocent in prison, and that just made me more angry. To live with that hatred was to live with the Devil. I needed a divorce! The only answer, my only salvation, would later be found in my love for my Savior and my salvation: Jesus Christ.

Prison was horribly and unpredictably violent. I think most people understand that. But prison violence isn't as simple as being the biggest toughest guy, or being ready to thump someone all the time. I know this might sound strange, but more often than not, prison violence is like playing chess. It's just that sometimes people don't know they're the pieces in a bigger puzzle, and other times guys just have a lot of hate built up inside and need to pop off, and you happen to be the guy walking by at the wrong time. That's why you need to keep your head straight all the time and understand what's going down, and also why you need to be prepared to go at any minute.

Most inmates with my conviction would have been offered PC–protective custody–but I wasn't, not that I would have taken it, because what was I going to do, hide for 45 years? I'd rather fight every day for 45 years, because I knew I was innocent, then hide in PC.

I knew how to defend myself from growing up on the streets, but prison violence is entirely different. Things happen quickly, so you have to be on constant alert. So I built my strength, and my speed, but so did everyone else. The one thing I learned quickly is that everyone is physically fit, and no matter how hard I trained or how big I got, there would always be someone bigger and stronger than me. But surviving a fight isn't about pure physical strength, it's about intelligence. You had to know who to fight, when to fight, where to fight, and how to fight. You had to know who and what to avoid, and most important how to conduct yourself in certain situations. I watched, listened and learned quickly. I saw guys that looked like giant oak trees chopped down by the smallest dudes, and I saw guys taken out in a matter of seconds with one punch.

Given all the constraints in prison—tights spaces, inmates and guards around, I learned that timing was the critical element in fighting. So I knew I not only had to be prepared, but I had to know when to be on guard. There were so many guys who didn't have control of their emotions who would fly off the handle at the slightest thing, and then suddenly find themselves fighting in a place that worked to their disadvantage. They lost their head, and they lost the fight. That doesn't mean you back down or don't stand up for yourself, but again, it's all a part of the bigger picture. Some guys will try to bait you, and what I learned is if you have to fight, you want to fight on your terms.

To help me stay fit, but maybe more to help me keep my head straight, I did crazy amounts of sit-ups, push-ups and dips every day. I did them so fast that I actually got a cardio workout. My goal was to do 500 push-ups in 15 minutes. At the end of the workout, my mind would be calm and my thoughts no longer racing, which kept me on top of my intellectual game; that, along with my physical strength, was my best chance at survival.

There were people serving in prison from all over Connecticut. Prisoners organize themselves by cities. So being from Hartford, I was associated with the Hartford crew. What's interesting is that guys from other cities, by far, were much more likely to call me a rapist and use that as a tool against me. The guys from Hartford, maybe because they knew me and thought I was innocent or out of respect for where I was from, would leave me alone. When I was in prison, there was definitely animosity between the cities, and sometimes it would bubble up into some pretty serious stuff. I found that the longer I served in prison, the more hatred there seemed to be between the cities, but I never felt it personally–I had enough to worry about.

I was always prepared for something, but that didn't mean I walked around in fear all day. But there were certainly places and times that were more dangerous, when I was on guard more. The shower was always a dangerous place. Packing so many guys into a tight space in a limited amount of time is kind of a recipe for something to happen, and as I mentioned mornings were also dangerous, when the doors were opened with masses of people moving through the block.

There's a place we all can go when it's a matter of survival–you just do what you have to do. During my most violent altercation in prison, the accumulation of rage flowed in me. It was like trying to put Niagara Falls through a garden hose. At some point, it had to come out. So my hose burst one day, ironically on a man who literally represented all the worst hatred in man. I'd have two years in solitary confinement to think about it. I was no longer that innocent kid from Hartford trying to make his way on the streets–I was now a man fighting for his life, but what was it that I was fighting for? Every encounter–every choice I was forced to make, helped me understand…

Chapter 13

FIGHT OR BE KILLED

There was a guy on my block who was well known as the leader of the White Supremacist group in prison. He would often make little comments to people to provoke them, which I let roll off my back. I knew he was trying to bait me into fighting. I also knew he was put in prison for assaulting kids–and literally stomping on them. This guy was a bad dude, and he kept a lot of people, his followers, around him for protection.

I was out at gym one day working out with a friend when I felt something awkward. I was near the weight bench when I stepped and lost my footing a little. Looking down, I saw a tennis ball near my foot. Not knowing where it came from, I grabbed it, looked up and tossed it out of the way. After I tossed it, I saw the reaction from the White Supremacist and I realized the ball came from his direction. I took note of it, but I said nothing and went back to my business. A short while later, the ball came back, again. This time I tossed it back directly to them, not throwing it hard, but sending it over a little more forcefully. The third time the ball came over, I walked away, leaving it there. I got tired of chasing this guy's ball, and I figured by now, this was more than just an honest mistake. This was a game for him—to have me fetch his ball. When rec was over, I made my way back to the block in the usual fashion, although I was certainly mindful of my surroundings and aware of where these guys were. I didn't want to be jumped, so I was tense and purposeful.

I knew I had to take action against this guy soon, because it was clear he was targeting me for some reason. If I failed to act and surprise him, my life would be in danger. Rather than waiting for the right moment, I had to make it. Back on the block, I was hanging with a bunch of guys and he walked by. "Hey Tillman, I do so much for you guys around here. Why didn't you get my ball?"

"I did get it…twice," I yelled back. "You know, it's my rec time, too. I'm no ball boy on a tennis court," I said loudly, walking towards him. The tension was high and I could feel myself losing control. "Fuck you, Rapist," he yelled back. I thought we might go right there—and I was ready for it, but it wasn't the optimal location—wide open, his people all around him, with people coming and going; it was easy to just move on. As I was walking away, I asked one of his followers, a guy I knew really didn't want to be with him, someone who was more reasonable, what this guy's deal was. He gave me information that confirmed my suspicions and hardened my resolve. "James, someone gave him a shank and he's going to cut you. Watch your back." The guy who gave him a shank was already serving 100 years in prison, so he didn't care if he got busted—I was worth it to him.

The next day when the lunch bell rang, I stayed back. I wanted to make sure I was at the back of the line. Not seeing me on the block, he did, too. I left my cell and started walking down the hall. I was a loaded cannon ready to blow. Boom. My elbow was nudged and I was brushed back against the wall–someone was trying to get my attention. The fuse was lit. The stage was finally set. He walked up to me, "I'm going to kill you, nigger." Being called a rapist was bad enough, but I had been called that many times before and I learned to deal with it.

However, being called a "nigger," by a guy everyone knew was racist just set me off. Tapping into a deep well of rage, I cocked my arm back and unleashed it with everything I had. He fell like a load of bricks. But I couldn't control myself, and I wasn't sure if he was going to get up and stab me, so I started stomping him. Bam, Bam! Bam! Bam! I just let loose. He lay there like a limp doll, so I kept pounding him. I kicked him so hard I heard the air being forced out of his lungs. I thought his guts might pour out. Interestingly, none of his guys tried to jump me. Finally the guards, who were standing back and watching this unfold, came and pulled me off him. They let me take him to the breaking point, and then they stopped it, saving his life, and saving me from a legitimate conviction in the process. I was sent to the infirmary to be checked out, and I walked down the hall like a conquering hero. "Way to go, James," people yelled. I turned a corner and a guard was standing there, and I thought, "oh shit, they're going to take me down," but when he came up he whispered in my ear and I was stunned. "Good job, Tillman. He deserved it." When I got to my room later that night, there was a huge tray of Chinese food waiting for me with a note. I didn't know what the heck was going on, and I was a little suspicious–maybe I was being set up, or was it left by accident? I couldn't figure it out. I walked over, a little tentative, and saw my name on a piece of paper folded in half. I opened it, and was filled with a sense of joy. I sat down, a huge smile on my face, inhaling the incredible array of Chinese takeout. The note read, "thank you Tillman."

But my heroics were short lived. After a brief hearing at the jail, I was transferred to Northern Correctional Facility–Connecticut's only

SuperMax prison, where I spent the next year and a half in solitary confinement for fighting–a punishment I deserved.

The truth is I don't like violence. I just wanted to be left alone. But I was serving in a place that breeds violence, and so I had to be prepared to live by the rules of the prison. This guy was going to kill me, so I had to be ready to defend myself. I hated what this man did to those kids, and I hated how racist and nasty he was. If there was anyone in prison I had to fight, I'm glad it was this guy. This situation also allowed me to again send the message: leave me alone–don't mess with James Tillman.

But maybe the most important message I took from this fight was personal: I realized there was still some fight left in me–that I wasn't ready to give up on life. I still hoped that my appeals could be heard by the Supreme Court, or that there might be some way to prove my innocence. At some level, I felt like I still had a life worth fighting for.

Chapter 14

SOLITARY & SUPERMAX

T here are prisons, and there are prisons that even the most hardened prisoners fear–that was Northern, Connecticut's only Super Max. Northern is considered a Level 5 prison–the highest security facility for the most dangerous offenders…and people like me who got into nasty fights.

There are three phases to life in Northern. Imagine a long rectangle with three sections and a large corridor going straight through the center of it, so you walk first through Phase 1, then Phase 2 to get to Phase 3 in the back. Most of Northern is separated by thick glass, so there's no place to hide anyway, but you rarely get that full glimpse of the place because you spent most of your time in the cell. Phase 3 houses Connecticut's Death Row inmates–people like Daniel Webb, whose arrest came just prior to my trial. Across from Death Row, there is a section where all the new prisoners sent to Northern reside. Northern runs a tiered program, so you start in Phase 1, and then with good behavior you get moved up to Phase 2, and eventually to Phase 3 and then finally transferred back to a Level 4 prison. Being sent to Northern is like being sent to the principal's office at school, except here the principal is Satan. So, I began my incarceration at Northern basically living on the equivalent of Death Row. In Phase 1, you are kept inside 23 hours a day. If you take rec, you are shackled with your hands cuffed behind your back and led to a door at the end of Death Row, which leads out to what amounts to a concrete pit—a sterile environment with four incredibly high walls and steel bars and barbed wire on top. It's like being in a cell that's flipped on its side and staring up at the sky. I could rarely take rec because I couldn't get my hands behind my back due to shoulder injuries and the size of my arms. I actually filed a motion to be allowed to take rec in Phase 2, but it was denied.

In Phase 2, the cuffs get moved to the front of your body, so once I earned my way to this level, I was able to start going outside to rec again. Seeing the sky again made me feel like I hit the lottery—how sick is that? In Phase 3, the big luxury is that you get to eat food in a cafeteria again.

You had 45 minutes in Northern for a shower and phone call. However, you have to shower with cuffs on your legs, which is kind of annoying. I looked forward to shower time, because it was the only time when I could see other people, especially since I didn't have my job as a Tier Man to fall back on at Northern. The physical isolation was very hard for me.

While much of Northern is glass, the place is very artificial and dark, because the cells had windows that were basically long narrow slits—about two feet high and six inches wide. It was more of a tease than it was a view of the outside. Looking at it sent me into fits at times, because I could never see a full tree. I always wanted to know what the rest of the world looked like out there. We were supposed to be in singles in Northern because the people were violent and many were flat out crazy, but because of overcrowding, we were doubled up. If you were going to get attacked at Northern, it would come at one precise moment: when you were cuffed to a bed and helpless. At Northern, whenever someone had to leave the cell, both guys would get cuffed to the bed. Then one guy would get un-cuffed and taken out of the cell, and then the other guy would get un-cuffed and remain in the cell. This allowed the guards to deal with one person at a time. 99% of the violent attacks at Northern came when one guy got cuffed to the bed. Despite having guards in the room, guys would just flip out on their cellies and beat the daylights out of them. They were already in SuperMax basically living in solitary, so what did they care? Guys that did this were always very careful not to touch the guards–it was kind of the unwritten rule. None of these fights lasted long, because the guys housed in Northern were such bad asses, they could take you out in a few punches–usually before the guards had time to react. So while I was living in Northern, I made my own rule with my cellies–I would never, and I mean NEVER, get cuffed first. My first cellie thought this rule was bullshit, so I offered to fight him right there for the right to make this rule, and he backed down. None of my other cellies questioned it. As a result, I was always cuffed last, but I never touched my cellies, which ensured that we could live in peace. I knew this wasn't fair, but I also knew I needed to protect myself.

After a year and a half of sitting alone in a dark box, I earned my way out of Northern. I was sent to Cheshire, one of the oldest, most run-down, overcrowded prisons in the state. It never looked so good to me.

Chapter 15

A GIFT OF LOVE

M y little brother Dennis was the light in my life. Every once
in a while you meet someone, and no matter who they
are or where they're from, you just kind of know: this is
a good dude. That was Dennis. Obviously I knew him well enough to
know that, but others who didn't know him that well would tell you
the same thing. He had some health problems, and he had a hard time
growing up in the city like I did, but to be with him you wouldn't
know that. He wasn't one to complain about his circumstances–he just
did his best–he was a positive guy and he didn't have a judgmental
bone in his body.

Dennis was a gifted teacher, although that wasn't his job. He
worked hard at a lot of jobs, including being a dishwasher at a
restaurant in Hartford. But it was a lesson he taught me one day in
prison that maybe stands as the most important lesson I ever learned
in life.

I was in my cell, a day like any other, just hanging out on my bed, staring at the wall. A guard came to the door, "Tillman," he barked, "you have a visitor." Surprised and curious, I made my way through the various check points to the Visitor's Center, wondering who it might be, because nobody from my family was scheduled to come that day. I turned the corner and made my way into the room, and there, waiting for me, was my brother Dennis–welcoming, but also serious, carrying himself with a sense of purpose.

"James, I've got something for you," Dennis said earnestly. He held up the check as if to make sure it registered with me. I couldn't believe the numbers. In fact, I did a double-take: it was for $1,100.

"Where did you get the money," I asked him, confused.

"I got it from my work, and I want you to have it. I want you to use this to hire the best lawyer you can so that you can get out of this place."

I sat back in my chair, totally blown away. I knew instinctively what I had to do.

"I don't want it," I declared, authoritatively. "I won't take it." I knew that he worked hard and that he didn't have much money, so I wanted him to spend that money on himself, to buy something he needed, rather than spending it on me, which at that time in my prison term was a waste.

"No, James, this is for you. I did this for you. I've been saving money and setting it aside for you. I want you to get a good lawyer and get out of here."

The emotions caught me by surprise. My hands shaking, my throat tightening, the tears starting to build. It took every ounce of energy I had to keep from balling like a child right there. I had to keep myself together.

"No, Dennis, I won't take it. That money is no good for me in here. It's too late for lawyers, but I'll tell you what: keep it and buy me a new pair of sneakers. I need a new pair of sneakers," I repeated, like I finally found the right argument that would put his generosity to rest. "Go get me a really good pair. That's what I need."

I didn't need sneakers, but I looked around at the other guys and noticed the brands. "Get me some Nikes." Anything in that moment to shut him down but also make him feel good about what he's doing. Every six months we were allowed to get new sneakers, so this seemed like a plausible idea to me.

Now it was my turn to shock him.

"Hey, Dennis. Thanks a lot man. I could really use those sneakers, but I've got to go. I'll catch you later." As quickly as I sat down, I got up and walked out, never turning back.

"James, our time isn't up!" Dennis protested. "C'mon, man! I want to hang with you!"

"I know, I'm sorry, I have somewhere I have to be," I said shouting back, without turning my head. I headed for the door as fast as I could without running. I refused to look back. I just kept walking. With each step, emotion started to swell. I hit the stairs and bolted up, moving as fast as I could.

"Open up, man. Open up," I yelled to the guard as I got to the door. The buzzer rang and it unlocked, and then I moved as fast as I could towards my cell. My feet pounding, my heart racing in rhythm. Boom. Boom. Boom. Boom. I couldn't get there fast enough.

I got in my cell, and thankfully nobody was around. I put the sheet up over my bed so that no one could see me, put my head in my pillow and cried uncontrollably.

Dennis' gesture was the most beautiful thing anyone had ever done for me, and it taught me a great lesson. On that day, in the misery that is prison, Dennis taught me everything I needed to learn about love. It wasn't the money at all. It was the countless hours washing dishes, scrubbing in dirty water, cleaning off the remains of other people's food. Night after night. Month after month. A few dollars here, a few there.

Money earned through hard work, dedication. True love is selfless—not the stuff you see in movies or find in greeting cards. Love is giving, sacrificing yourself for the betterment of someone else, without ever expecting anything in return. Love is doing your best for someone, no matter how imperfect we all are, or whether that effort yields $1,000 or $1 million. And true love is giving without any expectations—it is given for love—love is the act itself, not the end result. It's a lesson I hope I never forget, and it's one I'm grateful that I got from a Master Teacher, my brother Dennis. I had never felt love like that before. I didn't know what to do with it. I wish I could have stayed in that moment longer, let that love fill me up.

Chapter 16

HELL

A nother unremarkable day in prison. Same routine. Same place. Same clothes. I was sitting in my cell early in the day, fighting boredom. Another crappy breakfast, as usual, followed by a quick workout. And then, a surprise: I got back to my cell and found a note waiting for me. "Tillman, go to the chapel and call home," it read. I felt like throwing up. My legs started to get wobbly and my hands were shaking. I knew being sent to the Chapel for a call meant that something was really bad. What could it be? Was my mom sick? Confused, I walked towards the chapel, trying to read the guards faces as I made my way. Whatever was going on, they certainly didn't care. It was just another day on the job for them.

When I got to the chapel, I walked nervously up to the guard. "I got a note to come here and call home," I said haltingly, handing the note to him. He looked at me with indifference, and motioned me to the phone. Leaving me alone, I picked up the phone and called my mother.

"James, James," she said crying, so much that I could hardly hear her. She just cried and cried, and then, in between sobs, she just blurted it out, "Dennis is no longer with us. He passed away." "No, no!" I yelled. I wanted to scream, cry, burst, shout. I was in total shock. "No, this can't be," I kept repeating. "No, Mom, no!"

"Tillman, I have a shift change. Get off the phone now," the guard barked, sounding bored and uninterested. I didn't want to hang up. I wanted more information. I wanted to just talk to my mom, let her cry to me. I wanted to know what was going on. The guard walked over, "hang up now." "Please, let me talk to my Mother," I begged. "Not now," the guard said, dryly. "Hang it up, or I'll do it for you."

"Mom, I've got to go I'll call you back," I said, hurriedly hanging up the phone. The guard prodded me back to the block. I could feel my fists clenching in rage as I walked back to my cell. I could have killed that guy right there, but my thoughts were only on Dennis. "He's dead. I can't believe he's dead," I mumbled to myself. When I got back to the block, there was a lot of commotion, a lot of energy. Guys in the block were asking what happened. "My little brother's dead," I said evenly, in shock.

I sat there in my cell and I thought about Dennis and my mother. After all my mom went through, raising us, losing me to prison, and now this? Despite everything I endured, all the hell I was living in, I would have signed up right there for double my sentence to have just one more visit with my brother. Dennis was only 21 years old. I sat there taking it all in, and slowly the fact that my brother was dead began to sink in. "I'll never see him again," I said to myself. "I'll never see Dennis." I just sat there repeating it, as if I was trying to convince myself, like I kept breaking the news to myself again and again. That's the only thing I could think about. Being locked up was bad enough, but now this? I never got to be the big brother I wanted to be for him. I felt like I owed him that, and my time in prison robbed me of that opportunity.

Word quickly spread that something happened to me. Inmates walked by looking in, some with care, some with contempt. Whatever they were feeling, they knew to leave me alone. I knew I couldn't deal with being around people, so I just stayed in my cell. I also knew I had to maintain my composure–my public face, because even in this moment of grief, I couldn't show any weakness because someone might try to take advantage of me. Even in mourning, I had to be on guard.

I received a visit from one of the guys on the tier. "I'm sorry, man," he said, shaking my hand. "I'm out of phone time," I told him, "but I wasn't done with my call when the guard made me hang up." Prisoners are allotted a certain amount of phone time, and I had run out of mine, but I still desperately wanted to talk to my mother. I sat in my cell, broken, depressed, emotionally beaten down. I looked up out of the corner of my eye to see guys on the tier lining up to talk to the CO. I couldn't hear the conversation, but soon one of the guys came over to me.

"We're trying to convince him to let you have our time, James," he said to me, "but the CO said no." That news completely shut me down, I didn't talk to anyone, even if they came in. I went down to the chapel to pray, to have some time alone. The prison I was in was old, with automatic doors that seemed to take forever to open. As the door slowly opened, I exploded into a rage, unleashing a fury on the door, pounding the living shit out of it. Bam! Bam! Bam! My fist cocked and tight, slamming it repeatedly against the door. After unloading on the door, I was drained and exhausted. I didn't know which way to turn, what to do or where to go. I was scared and lost, like a rat stuck in a maze of emotion.

If there was a moment in prison when I reached my peak of hatred, this was it. I hated the guard for not letting me have more time to talk to my mother. I was utterly helpless. With every feeling I had, I wanted to break that man in half. My transformation was now complete. I wasn't the monster that committed the horrible crime against that woman, but my experience in prison had turned me into that monster, and in that moment, if I had the chance, I would have broken that man in two. I wanted to pour all my rage on him. To him, I was nobody, but to me, this meant the world.

The guards had a break and turned over, and I knew that was my chance to get on the phone with my mother. I approached one of the guards I knew to be fair, and explained the situation. Within minutes, I was back on the phone. "Mom, I want to hit this guy. He won't let me have more time with you. I want to break his face," I said angrily, emphasizing each word. "James," my mother said, shifting her tone and becoming more relaxed, "I need you now. I can't lose you, too. I need you to remain calm." I took a deep breath. The sound of my mother's voice, as it had so many times when I was a boy, instantly brought peace to me. "Okay, mom," I said. "I love you."

Dinner-time came, so I left my cell and made my way to chow. I ran into the same CO again, who confronted me, annoyed. "Trying to break the rules, are you Tillman? You know these guys can't give you their time." Clearly, he was trying to provoke me.

I knew if I reacted I wouldn't get a chance to go to the funeral or say goodbye to my brother, but I couldn't take it anymore. I knew I could take him out with one punch. I was at the lowest point of my life and I didn't ask for anything, except to be treated with a sense of fairness. Rather than snap at him, I held everything inside, stopped, looked him in the eye, turned around, and walked back to my cell, giving up chow. I didn't feel like eating anyway. On the worst day of my life, I wasn't given the simple courtesy of dealing with my grief by the guards at prison, but something else remarkable happened that day that I can only see now as an act of God's grace—the first building block in the restoration of my own faith, and reminder of the power of believing, the power of conviction… and it came from the most unlikely source.

Chapter 17

UNLIKELY ACTS OF GRACE

A ll of us experience death and loss—it's something we all have in common. Like everyone else who suffers a sudden, tragic loss, I was in shock. I sat alone in my cell, repeating the same thing, again and again: "Why, God? Why? I'll never see him again. Why?" Like everyone who loses someone they love, I was overwhelmed with grief. Unlike almost everyone else, I was experiencing this alone, in prison—the last place in the world where anyone wants to show any vulnerability. I couldn't comfort my mother, who must have been filled with inconsolable grief. I couldn't be there for her during what would become many lonely and heartbreaking days. I couldn't share stories of my brother with anyone. I couldn't laugh with them, cry with them or suffer with them. I wasn't just sentenced to 45 years. I now felt like I was sentenced to death. My life was complete loss, the loss of my freedom, the loss of my love. I lived in the shadows of humanity.

There I sat, in my cell, trapped, physically and emotionally, surrounded by oppressively thick, gray walls. I never felt more imprisoned than I did at that moment. Raw with emotion, I sat there alone for hours, lost in all my life had become. The arrest. The trial. The wrongful incarceration. The horrible start in that small jail. The hanging. The disgusting food. The bland colors. The awful smells. The lack of space and privacy. I felt myself tense up as I sat there. My mind started to race and my thoughts couldn't get off my brother. If I can't ever see my little brother again here, then maybe I can see him on the other side, I thought to myself. I want to see Dennis. I don't want to live here anymore without him. I wanted to die.

In that moment, for the first time in my life, I wanted out. How should I do it? I started to look around to see what I could use to kill myself. I had no reason to live. The darkness was so deep and the grief so strong, my only escape, I thought, was to go deeper into it and take my own life. I could find no reason to live.

Lost in my grief, my guard was down. I didn't hear the first footsteps until they were walking through the door of my cell. I snapped to attention, out of my haze, not sure what to expect. I intuitively tensed up, ready for a fight.

"I brought this for you," a guy said, looking me squarely in the eye, placing some food down in my cell next to me.

I looked up at him with my tired eyes. I began to let my guard down a little. "Hey, thanks, man," I said, sincerely, and then putting my head back down, losing myself in thoughts of my brother.

A few minutes later, another man came in. Again, lost in my thoughts, I didn't hear him. "Here, it's for you," he said, placing a candy bar next to the plate. "I thought you might need it." As quickly as he came in, he was gone.

"James, I got some chips for you from the commissary," another guy said, bringing them in and adding them to the pile building on my bed. A guard stopped by, poked his head in the door, "James, hang in there, alright?"

One by one they came, bringing me snacks or food, in their own way, checking on me to make sure I was okay, to let me know that they cared. They never said anything directly about my loss or about my brother, but I understood what was happening. It was a prison wake. I know it seems almost impossible, because prisoners are supposed to be scum in every way, but on that day I was reminded that in every person there exists the potential for God's grace. To those on the outside it might seem impossible, but even prisoners have honor.

I told myself on that day that the first thing I would do when I gained my freedom was visit my brother's grave; to remember him, to show my love for him, and in some small way to remember those who supported me during my darkest moment. Their kindness gave me a reason to live, if only to return the favor somehow, some way.

Chapter 18

THE DARKNESS BECOMES ME

I woke up earlier than usual, around 4 a.m., but the truth is I didn't sleep much at all. Most of my horrible experiences were surprises— my arrest, the conviction, the fights in jail, but this one—I knew it was coming, and there was nothing I could do except sit there in the gut-wrenching, awful pain and wait for it. Today was the day of my brother's funeral. It was nothing to look forward to, but nothing I could escape from either.

Time, that most precious gift to those who are living, gets all screwed up on days like this. Time stopped for my brother, but it was literally counted for me. Time moves slowly while I wait, and moves too quickly when I think of my last moments with him. Time, I'm not sure what it means anymore. I'm not sure what anything means anymore. My brother's dead and I'm burying him today, the rest of this world can just go to hell. That's what I thought sitting in my cell, getting ready for my brother's funeral.

There are moments of darkness and deep depression in life, and then there is the darkness itself. A gnawing, pervasive, festering, lurking, consuming darkness. It isn't something you think about, it's just something that is. It invades your soul and becomes you to the point where you start dying inside. And then that death, that darkness, it's how you mark life—the moments before someone died, and the moments after they died. That's what it's like for all those of us who have experienced this kind of loss. I was living in the darkness, and carrying it to my brother's funeral.

Most of my time that morning was spent with thoughts of him. Man, I just wanted him back, for one minute, just one more minute. I wanted to tell him all those things I never got to. I wanted to hug him one last time. I'd take another 45 years with no questions asked for just a few more minutes with him. But who was I bargaining with? I knew it was helpless, and so I just sat there, folded into myself, thinking of my little brother Dennis.

Death isn't just a moment in time, it's a process. It's a process that I'd normally be a part of—planning the wake and funeral, picking the plot in the cemetery, being with friends and family to comfort and grieve together—not just today, but for days, weeks, months and years to come. But for me, it's a process I'd be thrown into and then pulled out of, and I think that just deepened the emotions for me. All I knew, sitting there alone that morning, was that my mother was somewhere else, now locked in her own prison of grief. Mine was made of steel bars, hers was made of overwhelming sadness, and both were inescapable.

"James, it's time," the guard said to me softly. I was led to a room to be processed, where papers were signed and then the most inhuman of devices applied like some kind of bizarre suit. At home, miles away, family members were putting on their best suits, and here in prison I got dressed in stainless steel shackles.

We got to the parking lot and there was an unremarkable mid-size car. It's early spring, but I have no memory of the sunshine, the flowers, the birds or the blue sky–to me, everything was gray. One of the guards used to work with my cousin and knew him from Church, and he was very kind to me.

I got to the funeral home on Barbour Street in the North End of Hartford. The guards opened the door and helped me out. I stared at the building, anticipating what was waiting for me inside. My heart pounded with a mixture of fear and dread. People in suits walked by, not making eye contact with me. I walked in, turned a corner and saw my mom there in a chair, crying. Here it was, that moment, that unavoidable moment.

There was a set of chairs for the family, and then another set of chairs nearby for me, with a guard on each side of me. There were a lot of people there, but at that moment, it was like I was still alone in the world. People came in and out and talked to me, but I could only focus on my brother. As people walked by and then as the pastor spoke, I looked at him in the casket and I began to realize he was gone.

I sat in a chair thinking about Dennis. Thoughts of suicide again raced through my head. What if I made a break for it and they had to shoot me? I just couldn't imagine life without Dennis. At that time I hadn't given myself to God yet, but for the first time I entertained the thought that there must be a God, because for me to restrain myself and cope with all this, there had to be someone guiding me.

At the end of the service, we got up to leave. My mom came by and gave me a kiss and offered some comforting words, "take care of yourself, James." So that I wouldn't draw too much attention to myself or get in the way of anyone, I was the last one to get up and leave. I walked in silence, with a guard on each side of me. I got to the door, and a surge of adrenaline rushed through me. I couldn't leave. I couldn't take that last step. I hesitated and they stopped. I turned to the guard and pleaded, "can I please just see my brother one more time?" He nodded his head with a kind of caring look.

We turned around and walked back to the casket. With everyone else gone and the guards standing several feet behind me, it was just me and my little brother Dennis now. I walked to his casket, got down on my knees and lifted my hands up to pray. Tears streaming down my cheeks, I said my final goodbye to my baby brother.

"Goodbye Dennis," I whispered to him. I leaned over, put my hand on the casket for a moment and prayed, saying my final goodbyes. Now I was ready to go.

I stood up, tears streaming down my cheeks, walking toward the guards. We made our way back to the car with a heavy, thick silence filling the air. I never looked back. All I could hear was the sounds of the chains moving back and forth. Swish. Swish. Swish. Swish. It was an eerie funeral march.

On the ride back to Somers Prison, I stared at the ground. Usually time in a car was pure bliss—a prison vacation, with views of the outside world, long forgotten smells, views of people living life in motion. But for me on that day, I could do nothing more than just stare at the lines on the road as they moved by repeatedly. By the time I got back to prison, I was too tired to think about suicide. Having my brother's life taken away was so much worse than having my life taken away. If I questioned my belief in God, I believed in my brother and that his life had meaning. In the darkest moment, I found something to believe in. Losing Dennis literally forced me to question what I believed, and when it came to Dennis, there wasn't any doubt—just like the choice I made several years earlier when I was offered to cop a plea: I would choose to honor my brother with love. My choice, that day, was to live so that I could honor his life.

Chapter 19

THE APPEALS: MORE
DISAPPOINTMENT

Every prisoner that has a remote shot at an appeal will immerse themselves in the process. I was no exception. As my appeal became more real, I allowed myself to hope that the truth would, finally, set me free. But as the process unfolded, it was clear it wasn't going to go my way, and I could sum it up with one word: disappointment. My appeals came in two forms: a direct appeal to the Connecticut Supreme Court on issues involved in my trial, and a second appeal on what's known as Habeas Corpus, which involved the constitutionality of my imprisonment.

I held out so much hope for the appeals because I knew I was innocent, and I thought that if only the facts could be revealed, if only I could have a more fair trial–a trial where my side could be explained more thoroughly and with more conviction–that I would be free. I knew in my heart I would be freed, should be freed, so it was just a matter of counting the days to my appeal. But I quickly learned that's now what the appeal process is about. The legal system at that point wasn't concerned with whether or not I was innocent, but whether or not legal procedures were properly followed.

To assist in my appeals, I made contact with the UConn Law School, and they in turn connected me with Legal Aid. When I got to Somers Prison, probably like every prisoner, I started to think about my appeals immediately. I got screwed at the trial, but surely they'd figure that out during the appeal and I'd be freed, I thought. Unfortunately, it would be a couple years before I'd begin my work with the Legal Aid Society. Initially, my hopes were soaring, because Legal Aid told me about this new thing called DNA testing—new forms of tests that could tell with more certainty whether or not someone was connected to a crime. But these tests were not used very often. In addition, they weren't sure there was enough evidence to conduct a test. So, while they asked for and received all the evidence, at this point in time my appeal to the Supreme Court was going to have to come down to legal arguments, not DNA testing.

My case was heard by the Connecticut Supreme Court in September 1991. The Supreme Court has a rule that allows it to transfer appeals directly to it. My appeal involved a number of legal arguments, but there were three main ones involving the composition of the jury, the instructions given to the jury, and a set of pivotal notes taken by the police that should have been included in the trial.

On the first point, the composition of the jury, I felt strongly that I didn't have a jury of my peers. There were six members of the jury. Of those six, five were White and one was Hispanic. There were no African Americans, and nobody from the City of Hartford, where I was a resident and where the crime occurred. In fact, the jury pool—the group of people from which the jurors were picked—contained only two African Americans, and both were women.

I learned while in prison that my lawyer during my first trial should have argued against the makeup of the pool and pushed for a separate hearing about whether the jury pool was appropriate and whether the jury that was seated was representative. My lawyer also told me that the clerk was dismissing people from the jury pool for basically no reason, so it's hard to tell if my jury pool was manipulated or fair. In other words, it was difficult to determine whether I had a jury of my peers.

During the appeal, my legal counsel presented the following statement from me:

"Your Honor, I object to the jury array. I do not feel that this is a jury of my own peers and therefore it will be impossible for me to have a fair trial. Especially considering the facts of the Danny Webb case which has been in all the news and newspapers. And the fact that his case alleges that he attacked a middle class white woman from one of the suburban towns, which in fact is what my jury panel was made of. There were only two blacks from the entire panels in which I had to choose from. I'm sure that this doesn't comply with the statistical percentage of blacks for this geographical area. Therefore, this cannot be a jury of my peers and it will be impossible for me to have a fair trial. I therefore state for the record at this time, I would like to challenge the jury array and ask the court to order whatever is necessary for me to do this."

The court said they would not rule in my favor unless I could present evidence of discriminatory selection methods. During the initial trial, my counsel had what I would consider a casual conversation with the jury clerk, who was in charge of providing the pool from which the jury was selected. The jury clerk said that she excused many potential jurors for economic hardship because their employers would not pay the difference between their daily jury pay of $10 and what they would normally be paid that day. She did acknowledge that this could result in a "disproportionate number of minorities" being excused from jury duty. But because this was not formally argued in front of the judge, it wasn't considered a legal part of the trial, and therefore it couldn't be considered in the appeal–at least that's how I understood it. The court rejected my claim, stating:

> "The defendant bears the burden of making an adequate record to support a challenge to a jury array. All that this defendant ever offered to the court in support of his request for a new supplemental panel was his counsel's hearsay representations of a conversation he had with the clerk. The defendant did not offer the clerk's own testimony or any other testimony. He did not request an evidentiary hearing to support his claims, or a continuance in order to gather probative evidence. A challenge to a jury array will fail if the defendant presents no evidence to the court. A representation by counsel does not meet this evidentiary requirement."

The second argument for my appeal related to the instructions the judge gave to the jury. I thought this was my best argument. Specifically, we thought the jury should have been told that they needed to consider whether the victim was too physically impaired when selecting me as her assailant since she received such severe injuries to her head, specifically to her eye. As I wrote about earlier, as awful as the circumstances were, for a case that boiled down to the victim's identification of the attacker, I felt strongly that it was important that the jury understand that the victim may have been too impaired to make an accurate identification. At my initial trial, my requested instruction to the jury, which would have included providing them this information, was rejected. Instead, the Judge's instruction to the jury was as follows:

"You have had evidence from a witness making an identification of the defendant in this case. The factors to consider in making your judgment of the reliability of such witness in making that identification are: first, her opportunity to observe the person, how close, the amount of time, the lighting conditions, the degree of attention, and the degree of stress; second, her verbal description of the defendant as to consistencies or inconsistencies to the defendant; third the time which passed between the incident and the identification made of the photographs in this case and the in court identification made by her of the defendant; fourth, any incidents of suggestion as to which photo to select; and fifth, the certainty with which the witness identified the person in the photographs marked as state's exhibits C and D, and identified the person here in court."

When my case was reviewed by the Supreme Court, they acknowledged that the injuries the victim suffered may have affected her ability to make a proper identification. In their verdict, they said:

"Before the attack, the victim had been drinking. As a result of the attack, she received a cut on her left eyebrow that bled and later required seven stitches. Her left eye began to swell during the attack, and later closed completely. The entire left side of her face was swollen after the attack. Her right eye eventually became black and blue. Because she was hit in the nose, she suffered a nosebleed."

Because of this, the Supreme Court said that the trial judge could have given the instructions I requested, but they also said that the instructions given were good enough. They went on to explain in their opinion that even if the instructions were not good enough, a new trial wasn't required.

Relating to the eyewitness identification, I was frustrated that the Supreme Court didn't acknowledge the fact that the victim gave at least two descriptions of the attacker to the police, which called into question her ability to correctly identify her attacker. She told the officer at the scene of the crime that her attacker was "a black male in his twenties, approximately a hundred and fifty pounds. Height was unknown. Medium complexion. Fairly short afro, with long sideburns. Light colored clothes and a white Kangol hat." Three days later at the police station, the victim told the police that her attacker was "a black male, estimated height of five foot six inches to five foot ten inches, medium build, glassy eyes, wearing a baseball cap and a rust-colored jacket." I am five foot five inches tall, and I didn't own a rust colored jacket.

Strike two. The third pillar of my appeal to the Supreme Court had to do with the police detective's field notes. We argued that a pivotal note taken by a police officer during their initial investigation should have been included in the trial. As I understand it, field notes are literally notes that are taken by the police when they're investigating something. So as the police come upon a crime scene, they take notes based on what they observe. At my trial, I felt that the court wrongly excluded the notes as evidence. The police social worker's field notes recorded a conversation with the detective "to the effect that fingerprints had been found on the driver's side of the victim's car, but that they did not belong to the defendant." This woman was attacked by someone opening the driver's side door, where my fingerprints were never found, and there were police notes stating that, in fact, someone else's fingerprints were found, and this wasn't included at trial. At the trial the detective did say that the fingerprints were found on the passenger side of the car, but because the victim said the attacker only used the driver's side, this was deemed irrelevant. My lawyer tried to get the police social worker's notes used in the trial, but the prosecutor objected and the judge agreed with them. They were never admitted, and the Supreme Court rejected my appeal saying that "the defendant made no attempt to lay a proper foundation" to admit the notes.

In total there were five issues raised in my appeal. Of those, four were rejected because my lawyer failed to object during the original trial, yet I was told that my counsel met the standards for trial and my appeal couldn't be approved based on that. I don't get that–it doesn't feel right to me. On December 3, 1991 my appeal to the Connecticut Supreme Court was officially rejected. Justice Berdon was the lone dissenter in the case, and he is obviously a hero of mine. In his dissent, Justice Berdon wrote: "the defendant's constitutional challenge to the array must be reviewed as if these allegations of the defendant could have been proven at an evidentiary hearing." He wrote that he "would find, on the basis of the offer of proof made by the defendant, that he was entitled to an evidentiary hearing to attempt to make a prima facie showing that the jury array was derived in an unconstitutional manner." Only Justice Berdon was willing to give me a new trial, for which I will always be grateful. "There is a need to preserve public confidence in the fairness of a jury. That perception dissipates when the court, through its clerk, employs selection practices for the array that undermines the defendant's constitutional right to select a jury from a fair cross-section of the community."

When it came time for the Supreme Court to review my case, instead of looking at my case and asking: could there have been something wrong, I felt like the approach was to ask if the bare minimum was done to provide me with a fair trial. Based on that criteria, I didn't have a chance of being released on appeal. What I find interesting, and a little unsettling, is that my case is used in the legal process as precedent even though I was exonerated, which means a system that was admittedly broken only becomes more broken. As my lawyer said to me, we won the war and lost the battle.

My lawyer spent almost two years preparing my appeal to the Supreme Court. Since I wasn't allowed to go to the court, I heard about my loss in an almost cruel way.

Mail was delivered to your cell by having it stuffed through a small opening in the steel doors. I loved getting mail—all of us did—it was our only connection to the outside world. A day like any other, I was sitting on my bed in my cell. On this day only one envelope was delivered. It floated gently to the floor, near my feet. I picked it up. It was a thin envelope from the State of Connecticut. I looked at it and started to feel nervous. I knew this envelope would hold my fate. I looked at it for a second before I opened it. I'm told those who are applying to college have this same feeling of holding an envelope with your fate sealed inside, except the stakes were a little higher for me.

I opened it. I read the first couple words and knew instantly: my appeal was rejected.

"Damn it," I screamed, throwing the letter down and pounding the wall in frustration. I lay down in my bed with that old familiar feeling—horrible, depressing disappointment.

Chapter 20

THE LAST HOPE FOR FREEDOM

A few days later, my lawyer came to visit me. He reminded me that we were also filing a habeas appeal. Habeas corpus appeals were provided for in the U.S. Constitution as a way to protect an individual from unlawful incarceration. I figured if ever there was an unlawful incarceration, I was it!

Through the process, an appeal is filed to ask a prison official to bring the incarcerated person to the court so it can be determined whether the person was wrongfully detained. The petition has to show that the court ordering the imprisonment made a legal or factual error.

In my habeas petition, we argued that I had ineffective counsel for both the trial and appellate proceedings. I was crushed to learn that my petition was denied. The Superior Court judge, in issuing his ruling, said, "counsel's conduct falls within the wide range of reasonable professional assistance." The court did acknowledge that "prior to the petitioner's trial there had been considerable newspaper coverage of an assault on August 24, 1989 by an African-American male, Daniel Webb, upon a white female resulting in her death...Broad news coverage of the details of the Webb assault heightened the petitioner's concerns in regard to the racial composition of the jury panel available to serve as the petit jury in his case."

We decided to appeal this habeas decision. In this appeal, I made the case again that the trial counsel had been ineffective by failing to make "adequate offer of proof of unconstitutional jury selection methods." We noted that the trial counsel testified at the habeas hearing that he had questioned the jury clerk, and that he learned that there was a murder trial going on next door to our trial in which there "appeared to be a substantial number of black jury panel members...who would have come from the same array..." The trial counsel talked to the clerk, but didn't call for a separate hearing on the composition of the jury. The court concluded that the trial counsel's performance was sufficient, and even if it was deficient, that I had not suffered any prejudice.

Eight years after my first appeal, the Connecticut Appellate Court affirmed the rejection of my claims in state habeas proceedings. Once the Connecticut Supreme Court denied me the opportunity to make a last appeal, I had no more legal options. All hope was now officially lost. I was basically looking at spending the rest of my life behind bars for a crime I didn't commit. "I hate this place," I said to myself. "I hate everything." All along, I held out hope, a small glimmer of hope, that somehow this nightmare would end, that the system would recognize my innocence and I would be set free. But what could I possibly hope for now? Every time I started to believe that my fortunes could change, I was met by frustration and disappointment—time and again—like I was being tested. Knowing I had no more legal appeals, I began to lose hope. Could I ever believe in anything again?

Chapter 21

RAGE AGAINST THE WORLD

When you spend over 18 years alone in prison, like I did, you have a lot of time to think. Sure, I was tough and a physical presence. You wouldn't find me on the Block sitting and contemplating things, but when I was in bed alone at night, my mind wandered. That was the only place I could let my guard down. I spent a great deal of time thinking about the nature of suffering, and I would lash out at God. I'd ask Him, "God, why do I have to be here? Why do I have to endure this when you know I am innocent?" It was easy to take it out on God. He was, after all, the one who was supposed to have all the answers. Day after day, month after month, year after year, I'd struggle with this fundamental question: why did so many bad things happen to me?

Rather than find answers, I kept stewing over the same question, "Why me, God?" I gave my own answer through my attitude. Look at me the wrong way, and I was likely to take you out. That's the kind of anger I had. In some odd way, I think I could begin to better understand the men who served in prison with me. I don't condone or excuse what they did, but when you carry so much anger, you live life on an emotional fringe that most of the world can't appreciate. There's anger, and then there's a deeper level of self-destruction that possesses some the way I saw in that famous horror movie, *The Exorcist*. We send people to prison because they act like monsters, but it's in prison where the transformation is complete and you have to become even more of a monster to survive. It's an endless cycle of hopelessness and self-destruction. It's at this point where the anger has a hold on you, instead of you reacting in anger to certain situations, you are anger. The hate, the rage, it boils within and it erupts and comes out. It seethes out of you. You don't control it–it controls you. Your every experience can easily tap into that hate, even if it's something as simple as going to the shower and someone cutting in front of you in line. I was never angry like this before going into prison, but my wrongful conviction and my experiences in prison certainly found a way to bring it out. In prison, the world gets divided between those who carry this anger and those who don't, irrespective of your race or religion.

At this point in my prison life, I hated everyone. I got into enough fights to earn the reputation that I should be left alone. I was shifted from one jail to another. I served time in every Level 4 prison in Connecticut. I was raised by a very spiritual, religious woman. I walked into prison thinking I was religious, but I really wasn't. I was a Christian, but in name only. I was selfish. My experience with God went something like this: "okay, God, what are you going to do for me?" And when God didn't get me out of prison , I felt betrayed–as if that was the key component of the contract that secured my faith. When I didn't get the answer I wanted, I turned away from God and flirted with other religions–I pretty much tried them all.

I was lost, angry and at my breaking point. At this moment in the midst of my darkest time in prison, came my turning point. Typical of life in prison, it came in the form of a horrible fight. I was in Garner Correctional Institution in Newtown, Conn., and it was chow time, 4 p.m., on an otherwise unremarkable day. Many, but not all of the inmates in Garner, were there because they had significant mental health issues. And like every prison, there were a fair number of gang members. I guess you could say that this prison was a lot different than the others—it had an unpredictability to it that made me even more on edge. As is always the case in prison, there is a lot of chaos and a lot of noise when people are moving around and eating; people yelling, swearing. It's not like sitting in the cafeteria at your local school, or maybe it is! I sat at chow, by myself, my head down when I heard that unmistakable sound, a loud "smack," the familiar sound of a fist slapping against a face.

I turned around instinctively, bracing myself for an attack, as I always did when I heard that sound in prison, my body tense, and ready for anything. I looked up and saw a large Hispanic man just pounding on a black kid. I watched as one of the attackers grabbed the Black guy's neck with his left hand, and cocked his right arm back and stung him with a hard smack to the face. The victim slumped to the floor, and then a second guy came in with some kind of blade and cut his face while the third attacker cut him in the chest. There was blood everywhere, and the guy dropped to the floor like he was out, dead.

I looked around, and watched as the prison guards stood there. Nobody was going to do anything. "Bam, bam, bam," they were just pummeling him. Stomping him, beating the life out of this dude. Nobody was helping him. With every punch, all the noise in the room left. The room was totally silent, except the sound of flesh pounding flesh. It was then, I think, that my code kicked in, and without even thinking about it, I was leaping into the fight to save the little guy.

Racing up the stairs, my instincts took over. I ripped off my shirt (you never want to have any loose clothing on during a fight) and set my sights on the biggest guy. I went after him like a drone seeking its target. I literally launched myself at him, and I put everything I had into the strongest punch I could muster. I hit him square in the face, between his eyes, and brought him to his knees. I could tell he didn't expect it. This dude was tough—one of the toughest guys in prison, so I'm sure he wasn't used to getting smacked like this. When he fell to his knees, I pushed him to the ground and threw the knife off him and just started beating him in his face, again and again and again. Bam. Bam. Bam. Bam. Bam. I just lost it on this guy, pummeling him while the kid still lay motionless on the floor. "Whack," I felt a smack across the right side of my face. One of the other two guys got up and started punching me in the face. I knew if I stopped hitting the big guy, he would recover and start pounding me. So while I was repeatedly hit on the side of my face, I didn't budge and inch, and I kept my focus on beating the hell out of the big guy. I was so enraged and so focused that I didn't even feel the punches. Every ounce of rage and fury at the injustice I suffered was poured out in this fight.

Out of nowhere, a guy I knew jumped in and went after the third attacker, which gave me some relief—at least I didn't have to fight all three. It was now 3 on 2, and the victim started to get himself up. The guy I was fighting was so strong that as I was hitting him he slowly got up to his feet, and then we started going at it like two heavyweight boxers going toe-to-toe in some kind of brutal ultimate fighting match. I could taste the blood and sweat in my mouth as it gushed down my cheek. I didn't know how long I could last with the big guy, who by now was starting to fight back pretty hard.

The big guy then turned away from me and towards the other guy who jumped in. This was the signal that he was done with me, and he was now going to focus on an easier fight. Blood everywhere, inmates were now screaming. The silence that once covered the hall like a veil was now lifted. The prison guards, in a situation like this, kind of lay back and let the inmates go after each other until they get enough backup. As the additional guards came flowing in, they finally stepped in and ended the fight.

As I was standing there, trying to figure out where the guy I was fighting went, the smell of gas started to choke me. I didn't hear it get launched, but it was clear that a lot of it was used, because it consumed me very quickly, to the point where I had a hard time breathing and I felt like I was suffocating. I fell to the ground, grabbed my neck, wiped my eyes and grasped for breath. I saw one of the guards using mace, so I got up and ran to the other side of the hall and down the stairs, chasing the guy who punched me in the side of the head while I was fighting. He ran to get cover from the CO, which really pissed me off. Before this ended, I wanted a chance to hit him back. I figured I was in trouble already, so I paused for a moment in front of the guard, stared at this dude, and then reared back and hit the guy smack in the face. The guard was in a complete state of shock, and then he looked at me like he wanted to break me in half.

The next thing I knew I was flat on the ground, with bodies all over me. The guards pinned me down, and they stood on me with such force that it was hard to breathe. I desperately wanted to tell them, but I didn't have enough air in my lungs to speak. Finally I was able to squirm enough to yell, "I can't breathe." So they flipped me on my side, and I lay there, the reservoir of hate now exhausted. I don't know what happened to me that day. In retrospect, it is clear that I projected onto everyone all of my pain and anger, and that wasn't right. I started to think that I might die in prison. I finally reached a breaking point, and in that sense, this experience would prove to be a turning point for me. Sometimes in the midst of the most horrible circumstances, God shines a little light–enough to force a change. I was starting to crack.

Chapter 22

BROKEN

I was dragged down the hall by a mass of guards like I was a sack of laundry. The place was unusually loud, but I was so drained that all I remember was the rhythmic sound of feet shuffling. My eyes started to swell shut from the beating I took to my face, and as the adrenaline wore off, the pain got worse. An ominous steel door was opened in front of me, and then I was tossed inside. I crawled over to the cot, lay down and tried to focus my eyes on something to make sure I could still see. I was in as lifeless a place as any I've inhabited. Sterile and unforgiving in its bare cruelty, it was like sitting in a cold steel box. I lay there in solitary confinement, bruised and bloodied, wondering what was going to happen next. On the other hand, what did I care? What was the worst thing they could do to me? Make me spend more time in prison? I knew I was going to be punished, I just didn't know how.

I was brought before the guards for a hearing to answer questions about the fight. "Why did you do this?" they demanded. "I didn't think it was fair," I replied in an even tone. "Bullshit. Were you doing this for someone else?" they inquired. "No, I didn't even know the guy," I replied. "If this wasn't for a gang, and it wasn't because you were friends with this guy, did you owe him something?" they continued. "No," I said, "I just didn't think it was fair, that's all." They were incredulous. "You don't fight like that for fairness. What were you fighting for?" they pressed me, repeatedly, thinking I would break and given another answer, but I held firm to the truth. "I just didn't like the way it was going down. That's it." I replied. They stared at me in disbelief. "Oh come on, James," they pleaded. "Give us the real reason." It was clear they were perplexed. "I saw that guy getting beaten and I didn't think it was fair." With that they walked out, and soon I was given my verdict.

The guy who jumped in the fight to help me was transferred to another jail. My punishment: I was sent back to Northern, the Level 5 SuperMax jail. The dude who was attacked and the guys we fought were also sent to Northern.

Back in the old familiar darkness of Northern, I had some time to get to know the guy I defended, and you want to know something crazy? I didn't like him. I know it's nuts–I was sent to SuperMax for a guy I couldn't stand! While I didn't know much about the situation or what led to the fight, the attack just struck me as unfair because he was jumped. It could just as easily have been me or a friend. I'm the kind of guy who believes that if you want to fight me, look me in the eye and let's go one-on-one. But in this case, that didn't happen. I reacted out of a sense of fairness, driven by my code.

Shortly after our arrival, the guards came to talk to him. They told him that since he was the victim, he was going to be sent back to population in a Level 4 prison. He agreed to the transfer. I went nuts. Most guys, including me, felt he should have stayed in Northern as long as me, since I risked my life for him. That's part of the unwritten code we have. So with him gone, I found myself serving in Northern, alone, with the three people I fought. This wasn't a good situation.

My second go-around at Northern was initially more difficult, maybe because I knew what I was getting into, or maybe because I was just sick of the whole experience. I was back to being in my cell pretty much all the time without rec, because my arms were too damaged to get my hands behind my back for the restraints. I'd get into a cell, get comfortable with my cellie, and then they'd move me. They were bouncing me all over the place, and it was frustrating. I was tired, and sick of moving around and having to adjust to new people and new places. When I finally found a cellie that I liked, the guards came in and told me to pack all my things and get ready to move out. They were trying to break me. It was working.

During one of those moves, the guard walked to my cell door and opened it, standing rigid and firm. "Tillman, get your things, you're moving out." I sat motionless. He barked again, "Are you going to move? Get your things and get out of here, now!" I knew they what they were doing and I was tired of it, so I just sat there angry and quiet. I was done playing their games. "Tillman, get up!" he screamed.

"No," I said defiantly, but somewhat softly, expressing the sense of defeat and resignation I felt growing in my spirit.

"Tillman, I'm going to ask one more time. Are you going to get your things and get out?" the guard yelled at me. "Or do we have to do it for you?"

I sat there in silent defiance.

"*Fshhhhhhhh*," the spray immediately made me feel like choking. Without warning, the guard sprayed me with mace. I jumped up and flew into a fit of anger, screaming, punching, flailing at anything I could. The spray made me crazy, and I violently shook every part of me as if it somehow might mitigate the impact of the mace. I felt the familiar feeling of hands around my body, like an octopus' tentacles. Grabbing me, pulling me all over. I kicked, punched, shook my body, doing anything I could to break free, but my every motion grew more restrained. "Get off me. Let me go," I raged. No matter how much I tried, I couldn't fight back hard enough. There we so many pairs of hands on me. Slowly, but surely, I was dragged to my new cell and shoved on the cot.

"Tillman, shut up and lie down."

I struggled, but with less force. I was getting tired, and there were so many guards it was overwhelming.

I lay there on the bed, and felt something tighten around my left wrist. I looked over to see chains bundled on the ground, and before I could react, I felt the same horrible feeling on my right hand. I was being put in what are called four point restraints. In simple terms, I was chained and shackled to my bed. I struggled to get out, but immediately gave up. There was nothing I could do. I was pinned down so tightly that I could barely move.

The officers leaned heavily on me. Pushing me, punishing me. I was so lost in my hate I didn't feel the pain of their aggression in that moment. *Snap!* I felt the chains close tightly across my legs. There I lay, shackled and strapped to my bed, like a slab of meat.

Moment by moment, minute by minute, hour by hour, my sense of time and myself became blurred. Unable to move, my arms and legs began to writhe in pain. I was a beaten man, dragged to this horrific room and strapped to a crisp, clean white bed. After what I'm guessing was a few hours, I started to crack. For anyone who has endured physical punishment, it's easier to deal with it if you have a sense of how long it will last—you can kind of brace yourself for it. It's a mindset: 'I have to do this for a day so I just have to get through the next 24 hours.' When I got shackled, I lost my ability to understand how long it would last, so what I was experiencing genuinely felt like it would never end.

I was supposed to be released to eat and to go to the bathroom, but the guards somehow forgot. I felt that awful feeling of pressure, my bladder filling up. At first, it was easy to deal with, but as time passed, the pressure was so intense and it only fueled my anxiety. So I started to scream. "Hey I have to pee! Someone help me!" No response. "Hello? Guards! Hey guys, let me out! I really have to go!" I pleaded. No reply. The pressure was so intense it hurt, so badly that I didn't feel pain anywhere else. "Please let me out!" I yelled. "I have to pee. C'mon guys, I really have to go. I can't take it anymore." Silence. I stared up at the ceiling, as if looking away would somehow make this less personal. I groaned with relief as my clothes and the sheets soaked up the warm urine, which quickly turned ice cold and sickeningly wet. Tears of shame flowed down my cheeks as the urine slowly dripped off my bed and onto the cold concrete floor, drip by lifeless drip.

After a while, I mustered the strength to scream again. "Can someone help me? Please let me out so I can change. C'mon, this is wrong!" Again no reply. I was lying in a living coffin. A tomb, the most physically draining experience of all my time in prison. A short while later, I heard a sound. The door cracked open and a guard quickly appeared. Oh thank God, I thought. Finally, some relief–at least I'll get out of these sheets. I was so grateful. He put a tray of food on the ground near the door, and then walked out. "Are you kidding me?" I screamed. "This is bullshit. C'mon, man, you can't do this to me." As I lay there soaked in urine, hungry and cold, my food out of reach, along with, it felt at the time, my life. My body grew still and my mind returned again to thoughts of suicide. I was unable to move, and too upset to find any peace. Behind that hate and rage was a profound sadness. My life flashed before my eyes. I remember playing ball in the park, hanging out with friends at school, sitting at home with my brother Dennis, and going to church with Mom. How had my life come to this? I was exhausted, and I tried hard to keep my eyes open, as if I was afraid of what might happen if I fell asleep. And then, as I lay motionless, strapped to the bed, I gave myself the one thing they couldn't take from me: my ability to believe. "You can do this, James," I thought to myself as I slipped into a deep sleep. "You can do this."

While I slept, I was finally unstrapped, though I don't remember the moment of being freed. I woke up the next morning and had the chance to shower and change my clothes. From that point on, I didn't have any more problems at Northern. After a while, things became more "normal"–as normal as they can be in a SuperMax. When I was graduated to Phase 3, I went out for rec, and saw two of the guys I fought (the third had gone home). They had a couple more guys hanging with them, and I wondered what might happen. Would we pick up where we left off, or would we somehow let it go? They clearly had the numbers advantage now, so I needed to be smart. I decided to go to the rec yard with my head held high, not looking for trouble, but not broadcasting that I was an easy target. They didn't say anything to me, and I didn't say anything to them. After a few more times doing this, something really interesting happened. We found ourselves in the same area at rec, it wasn't like I approached them or they approached me, and I nodded my head and said hello, and they replied. The next time out, I did it again, and they replied and I came back with another word or two, and then slowly over time, we started to talk and when we got to know each other, we actually became friendly.

I remember sitting in my cell at Northern, thinking back on the fight and being strapped to the bed. Part of me felt deflated; people always let me down, but another part of me felt a firm resolve. No matter where I am, no matter what happens to me, no matter how other people act, people can take my freedom, they can take my possessions, they can take everything from me, except for one thing: my power to believe, to choose how I want to act and approach life. I wasn't giving up. In fact, I was in the process of summoning the faith to more forward.

Chapter 23

FREEDOM THROUGH FORGIVENESS

S till housed in the SuperMax prison, I was alone my cell next to what I can only describe as a monster–a crazy guy who was at Northern since its opening. He was so crazy he wasn't supposed to have a roommate, because it was well known that he would kill anyone put in his cell.

A young, slight guy, about 120 pounds, in Northern awaiting trial, got put in the cell with The Monster. Clearly, someone was trying to teach this kid a lesson by putting him in a cell with this guy. I heard the clank of the door closing and I squinted, as if I was watching something gross on TV. Almost immediately, like within seconds after the guard closed the door, I heard the muffled screams and the unmistakable sound of one person beating another. *Thump. Thump. Boom.* One pounding after another, quick and relentless. He was knocked out and beaten mercilessly, the kid didn't even put up a fight. *Clank*, I heard the sound of the door opening, and the familiar sound of a body being dragged.

Thankfully, he was still alive, for this kid, who was beaten like a rag doll, would change the course of my life.

When he was released from the infirmary, he asked to be placed in the cell next to me. We started talking, and it turned out he knew my family. He clearly had made bad choices in his life, but he was more like a lost kid–he would have been a lot better cellie than most of the other people at Northern. I was judged by the label society put on me– convicted rapist–not for who I was. So I live strongly by Matthew's words in the Bible, "judge not lest ye be judged." We are more than the labels life puts on us. So, I decided to talk to this kid and take my own measure of him.

He told me that he heard about my trial and the deal I was offered, and he asked me why I didn't "cop out," take the deal that was offered. "Because I'm innocent," I said to him simply, as if I was describing the color of paint on the wall. I think he could hear the sincerity of my tone. For reasons I'll never understand, these words stuck with him, and would one day build like ripples that would rise into mighty waves and crush walls of indifference and inhumanity; words that would one day change the entire course of my life, but there, in that moment, we were just two guys talking.

He was considering copping out, taking the light sentence in order to avoid the hassle of a trial. I told him he should do what he felt was the right thing, but I reminded him that, "you have to live with this choice for the rest of your life." When it came time for his trial, he went to the judge and told him that he was considering copping out. The Judge told him that if he thought he was innocent, he shouldn't cop out, and in fact the Judge said he wouldn't let him. He sat there thinking of his conversation with me, which he said inspired him, and so he stood his ground and didn't cop out. Like me, he was headed to trial.

Before his case was heard, his mother gave him a Bible and told him to read the psalms, pray and really think about what they meant.

So we started reading psalms 20, 23, 35, 70 and 91 together. We'd stand there, in our cells, taking turns reading to each other. "The Lord is my shepherd; I shall not want. He maketh me to lie down in green pastures: he leadeth me beside the still waters. He restoreth my soul: he leadeth me in the paths of righteousness for his name's sake. Yea, though I walk through the valley of the shadow of death, I will fear no evil: for thou art with me; thy rod and thy staff they comfort me. Thou preparest a table before me in the presence of mine enemies: thou anointest my head with oil; my cup runneth over. Surely goodness and mercy shall follow me all the days of my life: and I will dwell in the house of the Lord forever."

A while later, after reading the psalms together for days I was sitting alone in my cell. This day wasn't any different than the others. I had my thoughts, and not much else. "Tillman, got something for you," the guard said plainly. To him, it was almost an annoyance to be dealing with delivery of something, but to me, getting anything was like Christmas a million times over, it was so unbelievably cool. I looked down at what I held in my hands. It would turn out to be one of the greatest gifts I ever received. It was my friend's Bible.

By the time I got the Bible, I had lost visitors, phone calls and commissary. I was isolated in a SuperMax prison whose purpose was isolation. I sat in my cell, 23 hours a day. I had nothing to do but read the Bible. It was basically the only thing I had left in the world to call my own. I had lost my faith in man, and despite my isolation, I somehow connected to a guy at rec–a guy I trusted–who had given his life to Christ. "James, read the Bible, but this time don't read the words, let the words sink in. Think about what God is telling you. Don't just read it, learn from it and live it." So I started to read the Bible and really get into what I was reading, and it just started clicking with me. As my faith in man waned, I was slowly restoring my faith in God. I read the parables about Jesus and the lost sheep, the lost coin and the lost son. Each story reflecting God's concern for lost people, the tremendous value He places on every individual. In each parable, Jesus shows us how much joy there is when each is found. I was moved by Jesus' lessons to his disciples: "Do not judge, and you will not be judged. Do not condemn, and you will not be condemned. Forgive, and you will be forgiven. Give, and it will be given to you. A good measure, pressed down, shaken together and running over, will be poured into your lap. For with the measure you use, it will be measured to you." (Luke 6:37-38). "Forgive and you will be forgiven." What an incredibly powerful expression. Forgive. I couldn't shake that concept of forgiveness. By reading the Bible, I started to connect to something bigger than me. I had unknowingly reached my turning point. My foundation was cracking open. Soon, it would be blown up, and upon it a new, much stronger, house would be built.

I woke up early. It was a day like any other that I had spent for year after year after year after year. Except on this day, I felt different. I didn't want to get out of bed. We all have days like this, but for me, it was deeper than just being comfortable and not wanting to move, or feeling a little sick and wanting to rest. I felt dark, down, depressed. Not angry, just out of sorts. Do I have to do this again? I just didn't want to get out of bed.

I turned away from the door so that nobody could see me. I felt overwhelmed with emotion. I felt listless, heavy, like I had weights on my hands. I reached over and grabbed my prison uniform, staring at it. I held it in my hands and clenched my fists. Tears started to run down my weathered cheeks, and then they poured like rain as I sat holding myself. Alone in prison, in a sea of despair, the life in prison had finally overwhelmed me. I was tired. Tired of the prison uniform. Tired of the food. Tired of the routine. Tired of using the toilet out in the open. Tired of having no privacy. Tired of the bed. Tired of rec. Tired of missing my family. Tired of the small, confined spaces. Tired of missing my brother. Tired of not having any kind of freedom. Tired of not seeing the light. Tired of not being able to take a walk. The guards spent years trying to break me, but I remained strong. Now, lying there, I was cracked wide open. I wanted to die. I turned my thoughts to God, but this time the tone would be different. I wasn't angry at God, I was confused.

"God, you know I'm innocent. Why do I have to serve here? Why do I have to suffer so much? If you are truly God, then please tell me why I am here?"

I didn't leave my cell all day. I lay in my bed. Too tired to move. Too tired to eat. In jail, you carry yourself with authority, or you become a victim. But I knew I couldn't carry my head high. Not today. I just had no strength left. I didn't even have the strength to fight with God anymore as I did all these nights awake in my cell.

I stood up and paced around. I thought for a moment about all the psalms I read. I reflected on the life of Christ, how he suffered and gave so much of himself for others, particularly the less fortunate, in other words, he spent his life caring for people like me. I thought about Colossians 3:13, "bearing with one another and, if one has a complaint against another, forgiving each other; as the Lord has forgiven you, so you also must forgive." There it was again: forgiveness.

I sat down on my bed, the mattress heaving with the steadiness of my solid frame. I placed my forearms on my weary legs and folded my hands in prayer. I sat there, in the darkness of my 10 x 8 cell, and opened myself to God, but this time, I decided to speak directly to Jesus Christ using words I never uttered before. "Jesus, please forgive me. I am where you want me to be. If you want me to stay here in prison, I'll stay and accept it. I understand that this is the life you have chosen for me. I will not try to change it or fight it. Just please give me my strength back. Teach me how to find love again. Teach me how to be strong, and to let go of all these things that have possessed me. Let me represent you and I will serve you until my dying day." And then, out of nowhere, I said the words out loud that solidified my new direction. "I forgive…" I forgave the accuser by name. I forgave the detective. I forgave the guards who had punished me, by name. I forgave my fellow prisoners. I forgave the judge. I forgave the jury. I forgave my attorneys, and then I closed with one final appeal. "My Lord and Savior, Jesus Christ, please forgive me."

I lay back on the bed and tears flowed uncontrollably. In a cold, dimly lit, smelly, disgusting room, folded into myself on a thin uncomfortable bed; in the most improbable of places; in a SuperMax prison in Northern Connecticut, in the dawn of a day, the dawn of my new life, I genuinely felt the love of God for the first time.

That love, in that precise moment, transformed me.

Where there was once hatred, I sought love.

Where there was once judgment, I sought forgiveness.

Where there was once war, with myself, with my fellow inmates, even with God, I now found peace.

In that moment, with each tear, 17 years of hatred poured out of me. I couldn't hold on anymore. I felt overwhelmed. It was like I was standing at the edge of a cliff, feet almost falling off the edge, holding on by a loose thread. My body was exhausted, ready to give out at any second. I felt the thread snap, and saw myself slowly falling over the edge. I didn't reach for help, I just tumbled over and over. I let go, and held onto the shred of faith that would become the fabric of my life. I sat there in bed, replaying that image in my mind until I fell fast asleep. I woke up around dinner and just lay there praying. "Let me find love, God." I have no idea why I was saying those words, but it was my impression of how Christ lived his life. There is no doubt he struggled mightily, but his every purpose and action was taken in love, and I thought if I could just be connected to that loving spirit, I would be okay. I lay back down, closed my eyes and mumbled my way to sleep in prayer. "Help me find love, God" I faintly whispered to myself, "help me find love."

The next day I woke up, feeling incredibly strong. I thought I was dreaming. It was as if my jail cell became a luxurious hotel room. I said to myself, "this must be you, God." After lunch, the guard came to my cell. "James, you have a visitor," he said dryly. This was unexpected, and I wondered who it could be. I was led to a small room arranged with thick Plexiglas walls. I sat in a cubicle, picked up the phone, starting at the two people on the other side, wondering who they were and what could be going on. They looked serious. A man and a woman, middle aged, staring back at me. I read the tension in their faces, and in looking at their posture and manner, I could sense a certain energy about them—they weren't passive or relaxed. Probably not from prison ministries, I thought.

I picked up the phone with some hesitation, not because I didn't want the visit, but because I just didn't know what was going on. It was then that I heard the sounds of my guardian angels.

"James, I'm Karen Goodrow, and this is my colleague Brian Carlow. We're from the Connecticut Innocence Project, and we're here to talk to you about your case."

It was a miracle.

Chapter 24

CONVICTION

My mother came to visit me shortly after Brian and Karen left. I walked in the room and sat down, just like I had so many times before. She sensed something, and immediately came after me.

"Son, there's something new about you. Something different."

"No, Ma, I'm still the same guy," I said.

"No son," she said, arguing with me, "Something is different about you."

"No, Mom, nothing's different," I demanded. Just because I found Christ didn't mean I had to stop arguing with my mother.

I checked myself and leaned in to her. "Mom, I gave my life to Christ," I said solemnly, confidently.

She started to cry. I started to cry. I wanted to hug her but I couldn't. I could feel that pride in her. My attitude changed. The COs and guards started to notice. It felt good to feel again. It had been years since I felt that way. It felt good to feel pain for someone. I felt bad for my mom having to come all the way to visit me. A kid came to me who just got hit with a 60 year sentence, and I remember feeling bad for him. It felt so good to feel empathy again even if it was a bad situation. Most of all, it felt good to love again.

Seeing and knowing that I was carrying myself differently, one of the guards came to my cell. "Hey James," he said, "I want to ask you to do something. Would you pray for some of the guys here who are having personal problems?" "Sure," I said, "I'd be honored to." Imagine, a cell mate being let out of a cell to go a pray for another inmate. How bizarre!

As I was walking along the hallways of the Supermax prison, I remembered words spoken to me many times at Church, these words now had significant meaning to me: God doesn't give us any more than we can handle. I felt like I could handle anything now. I realized now that God was completing his process and that he had just released me from my own prison. I was so grateful, and I now realized why I had endured the wrongful conviction and all the suffering. I did it so that I could find my way back home, to the salvation that exists only in relationship to God.

I joined the choir and Bible studies. I started coming out with my Bible and talking to young kids, kids with sentences of 70, 80, 90 years. When I was released from the SuperMax prison, I found myself in a cell near the showers. There are always long lines to get into the shower–the result of having a lot of inmates and few showers. I took advantage of my audience and I started preaching to people, very loud. I figured if they were going to give me all their gang talk, I'd give them a little talk about Jesus. "Shut the hell up, Tillman," they'd yell. I just smiled, laughed and talked louder. "Oh, okay, you can't hear me. Let me be a little louder…" I wasn't expecting to convert anyone, but it was fun and it certainly couldn't hurt. "Jesus loves you," I'd yell. "You can find salvation in Christ."

Rather than sit with my hatred and wait my turn to take a shower, I took advantage of the opportunity to reach out through the walls of my prison cell. Some of the guys were really annoyed at me, but I didn't care. I kept my focus on loving God. I noticed that my life started changing once I started to love others. It felt so good. I was now ready to die for this. Mine was a transformation on two levels. My mindset, my attitude, changed when I accepted Christ, but the biggest and hardest transformation came with the choices and actions I faced moment to moment, day to day. It's one thing to say: I love God, but if you then make a choice to react with hatred when someone curses you out, which happens on a regular basis in prison, then you haven't fully given your life to Christ. We are all human, and so we make mistakes, and I continue to make my fair share of them, but when I gave my life to Christ in prison, I gave tremendous energy to making the right choices and taking the right actions. Up to this point in my life, I had survived by following my own code, and it served me well, but only to a point. It kept me alive, but it also prevented me from truly living. Now I was following God's code, and I was free, but it took a lot of work, especially in prison. It was only because I had all the years of experience in prison that I was able to understand and value this new code based on love. This was the ultimate gift that came through the power of forgiveness. Where I would normally react with anger, I found empathy. "Hey James, screw you, man" someone would yell. Instead of saying something back that would leave me on the edge of a fight, I would either say something more kind in return: "hey Jesus loves you," or I would just ignore him. I realized that his comment was more about his pain and frustration than it was a judgment against me.

But giving my life to Christ didn't mean I stopped fighting. In fact, the fight I'm most proud of came after my transformation. When I gave my life to Christ, I felt the need to be baptized. I was baptized as a young man, but I obviously don't remember any of the details, and I felt

I needed this baptism to signify my transformation. If I had to spend the rest of my life in jail, I wanted my experience to be marked by my immersion in a baptism tank, the same way Jesus was immersed in a river. Unfortunately, Cheshire Prison didn't have a baptism tank. I asked the CO if we could get a tank, and I was told, very clearly, they wouldn't do it. I think they felt since I gave my life to Christ that I would be easier to control and I would be more submissive, but I came back at them hard. Rather than using my fists and my rage, I used my mind and my heart for this fight. I sat in my cell, thinking hard, writing and re-writing a letter. I acted as my own legal counsel, and used my best arguments to petition for a tank by filing a formal grievance. I formally requested that the baptism tank be constructed at Cheshire, and my request was summarily denied. They thought the fight was over, but I went back at them again. I filed an appeal. Unlike in the past, I felt the power of Christ with me. I also had secret allies in some of the guards. In fact, one of them whispered to me during this fight, "keep it up James. Don't give up." I was denied a second time, and then a third time. Instead of meeting my denials with anger, I met them with resolve and love. I revised my petition, and submitted it a fourth time, and curiously did not get an immediate reply. A few months later, the reverend called me down to the Chapel.

"James, I'm going to need your help with something," the reverend said to me. "Sure. What can I do?" I thought he wanted me to talk to another inmate about the value of letting go the hate and giving your life to God. "James, I need you to help me build this," he said, smiling and stepping away from a large crate. "It's our baptismal tank." I hugged the reverend, and took a moment to pray and thank God. This was one of the best days of my life.

I started to go to church. I started to take care of others. I joined the Bible study and choir. I was resigned to the fact that I wouldn't be helped by the Connecticut Innocence Project, but if they took my case

I at least I had a shot at getting out. My focus was on serving God, not myself. I was more focused on that than I was on being freed from prison. In some ways, I was already free from my own prison of hate.

My life in prison wasn't perfect after I accepted Christ, and I think, especially for young people reading this, it's important for me to admit that. Sometimes we make bad choices, but we have to try to discipline ourselves to understand our choices, take responsibility for them, and resolve to continue to act in a Christ-like way. Choose love over hate. Choose forgiveness over indifference. But I have to admit there was a time when I found myself reacting in my old ways. I was continually being harassed by a fellow inmate and one day, at the end of the verbal abuse, he called me a "nigger." I just instinctively reacted, turned, and punched him. "Whap," I took my left hand and held him down and I started to pound him, punching him in the face. "Bam, bam, bam," I pounded on him like a jackhammer. I unleashed on him so strong, others, I think, were worried that I might kill him. Unlike in the past where the guards let things go before jumping in, a guard who I knew walked with Christ and knew of my transformation, jumped on me. He whispered in my ear, "James, you are with Christ. Let him go."

I heard the voice in my head and it was like flicking a switch.

I backed off. The guards slammed me against the wall, and then I found myself again in solitary confinement, a prison inside a prison. I deserved my punishment. I prayed for forgiveness, and I thanked God for the guard, who saved me from doing anything that would have resulted in a longer prison sentence and a rejection of my appeal.

What I realized after that incident was that I had found freedom in my life through Christ. I would never again make the choice to turn to hate and anger, because it felt so good to finally be free.

Chapter 25

A GLIMMER OF HOPE

I didn't learn until later that my case was brought to the attention of the Connecticut Innocence Project by the guy I befriended who loaned me his Bible. He was convinced of my innocence and lobbied the Innocence Project. I could have stayed in my cell, comforted by my anger, shut off from the world. If there is any lesson to be learned from my experience it is this: when you give yourself to God, and you act with love, anything is possible. Sometimes, random acts of kindness really do change the world. I reached out to someone, and that small gesture led to him going to the Innocence Project on my behalf. Maybe sometimes seemingly random and insignificant acts of love really can change the world. I didn't stand there talking to him thinking, "what am I going to get? What's in this for me? How can I get food out of him," or something like that. I stood there, listening to him, feeling his pain and then counseling him. I offered him my advice and my support. He later told me that when he felt my innocence. It took another prisoner to see something in me that very few people did—that I was innocent. Unbeknown to me, upon his release, he wrote the Innocence Project, urging them to take up my case.

The Connecticut Innocence Project was formed in the summer of 2005 by former Chief Public Defender Gerry Smyth. Attorneys Brian Carlow and Karen Goodrow were asked to Co-Chair the Project. Gerry, Karen and Brian are true heroes of mine, and they continue to inspire me. Brian's expertise is DNA, and Karen's passion is wrongful convictions. Smart, passionate, loyal, determined, they are everything an innocent person could ever want for counsel, and for friends. I liked to call them my Dream Team—basketball had its Pippen and Jordan, or LeBron, Wade and Bosch—and I had Karen, Brian and Gerry. What I find remarkable is while they were working with me, Brian and Karen were also working full-time in other positions within the Public Defender Division. Most people like to spend free time reading a book, watching TV, or just hanging out. Karen, Brian and Gerry spent what little free time they had working on behalf of those they felt had been wrongfully convicted. In our world today, so many people, especially kids, look up to rap stars, musicians, movie stars. All they have to show for their life is their celebrity and their work, which is fine, but it's all about their glorification, not the public good. If what happened to me represents some of the worst in people, then the people that do work like Karen, Brian and Gerry represent the best. We would be much better off if kids looked up to people like them. You might say that a few hours spent on the Connecticut Innocence Project a week might not seem like a lot, but for someone who's innocent and stuck in a prison cell, it's awesome.

As you can imagine, the Connecticut Innocence Project is flooded with requests, so my case wasn't investigated immediately. That I even made it on their radar screen is a miracle in its own right, considering the number of requests for representation they get.

Thankfully I had already submitted my own information to the Connecticut Innocence Project in January 2005, through my own letter and forms, so when the released prisoner wrote them and they looked in my file, there was enough information there for them to take the next step in the process: a meeting with me.

Brian and Karen came to visit me on what I'm told was a cold, gray day in February 2006. To me, every day was cold and gray! They came not to tell me they were formally taking my case, but to talk to me and tell me they might take my case. I was nevertheless ecstatic and overwhelmed at the chance that justice could finally be done, after I had given up any hope of release. Brian explained to me that because DNA testing wasn't done in 1989 when I was convicted, and that the DNA testing that was done in the early 1990s was so crude, there was potential in my case because DNA testing as we now know it was very advanced, and was not done in my case. They explained to me that if the DNA evidence proved my innocence, we would petition the Court for a new trial. In cases where DNA is used to test evidence, there is no statute of limitations, which means I could go back to court at any time in my life. Incredibly, Karen told me that there is a 3-year statute of limitations in cases where there is no DNA evidence involved, and that only about 10% of the wrongful conviction cases involve DNA. I was so grateful that mine met the criteria and that the DNA evidence could be tested, but I wondered what it meant for someone who is innocent and doesn't have DNA. I was told that even if my innocence was proved, the Judge would have to agree to a new trial if he determined that the new physical evidence would have made the verdict different. To get before the judge, however, we needed the prosecutor, Ed Narus, who was the person who put me behind bars in the first place, to give his consent to going back before the judge. It's important to note that the DNA evidence doesn't automatically grant immediate freedom—just a new trial. So if the DNA evidence found it wasn't me, it would be as if I was walking into the courtroom for the first time after I was arrested, 18 years earlier.

But the purpose of their visit wasn't to talk legal process, and it was anything but a technical conversation for me. While Karen and Brian hear from a lot of people about cases, before they will take on a case they want to meet personally with the person wrongfully convicted. They left our first meeting giving me the single best gift I have been given in my life to that point: their faith in me. "James, they said to me, "we're willing to take on your case."

I could feel the phone loosen and shift in my hand, like I was holding a 20 pound weight and then given a 2 ounce one. As those words sunk in, I felt a surge of adrenaline rush through my body, and then I kind of went limp. I had a really bad night the night before, so I was kind of at the end of my emotional rope walking into this conversation. At first, all I could do was cry. I just cried. "Praise Jesus," I repeatedly whispered to myself through my tears. "Thank you God." As they left, I sat there, trembling, wanting to scream with joy. I was sky high emotionally. They turned, walked out the door, into freedom. I composed myself, turned, and walked back into the depths of Cheshire Prison, a growing appetite for freedom building, and burning inside me.

Karen and Brian began searching for evidence on February 23, 2006. You tend to remember dates like this when you're confined to prison for 18 years. If my case was to be based on new DNA evidence, then they needed to find the evidence to test. Given that the evidence is kept in a vault monitored by the State, getting it should have been a very simple procedure.

I was pacing around my cell, so excited to see Karen and Brian again, looking forward to hearing good news about my case. I made my way up to the Visitor's Center carrying myself with amazing strength–like a force was propelling me. Step by step, one step closer to freedom. When

I got to the Visitor's Center and saw the look on Karen and Brian's faces, I knew they weren't there to give me good news.

"James, we can't find the evidence," Karen said in an even, professional tone. "What?" I replied, stunned and shaken. How could this be? She explained that they exhaustively tried to find it, but it wasn't where it should have been. She said they would continue to work on my case and keep looking for the evidence, that they wanted to help me, but without conducting DNA tests on the evidence, there wasn't much they could do. The state basically lost my evidence. My freedom was held in the balance by a very thin thread, and on the other side of that thread was the state's bureaucracy. Unbelievable.

Chapter 26

EARNING REDEMPTION

nother devastating blow. No evidence, no case and no hope of release. I felt really bad, but as I got back to my cell, I prayed. "God, if this is how you want me to spend the rest of my life, I'm prepared for it. I am innocent, but I am also your servant, and if you want me to serve you here for the rest of my life, I will do it and I will be strong. I am willing to die here." I had my strength back, and I knew I could do this, I could spent the rest of my life in jail if I had to. I came to terms with the fact that I was never going to go home. "With you, God, I have the faith to move forward." I carried myself with strength. I refused to let the bad news get me too far down. I refused to use this as an excuse to turn away from the Lord, and back to a life of hatred and anger. I had a quiet resolve about me. I came to feel almost settled in a strange way–that I had final resolution on my case, and began to face the prospect of finishing my term in prison. I was no longer a man looking forward, with the hope of a release, but one in the moment, guided by a higher purpose. I continued to attend church and Bible study. I continued to heckle fellow prisoners at the shower. And I continued to be an antagonist, in my own loving way, for Christ.

I was sitting in my cell, passing time and reading the Bible when the guard came to me. "Tillman, you have a visitor." I knew it was my mom or Brian and Karen. When I got up there, I could just tell from the look in their eyes that there was good news. "James, we found the evidence," they said. What they didn't say was how they found it. The story is amazing.

During my 1990 appeal, I had enlisted the help of Legal Aid. DNA testing at that time was still relatively new, so when the evidence was tested the results weren't conclusive. They also never tested the crotch area of the victim's underpants, which explains why there wasn't enough material to get a definitive result. Back in 1991, the protocol was to not test highly saturated areas, which in light of what we know now seems kind of bizarre. Now DNA tests can be conclusively done with miniscule amounts of evidence. In 1991, the judge ordered the evidence sent back to Life Codes, where it had been kept during my appeal proceedings. Normally all evidence is returned to the State Vault, but the judge made an innocent mistake, and one that would eventually work to my benefit. What I faced in my case was almost a perfect storm of screw-ups.

Karen, not an assistant or legal associate, took personal responsibility for tracking down the evidence. She made repeated calls and wrote letters. She worked exhaustively, talking to about 25 people in order to determine the trail of my evidence. She told me that she never would have found the evidence without the unexpected kindness of strangers–people who didn't have to do anything for her or for a convicted rapist in prison. One of the turning points in my case, ironically, involved the police who wrongfully sent me to prison. Karen was able to find one of the policemen involved in my case. He didn't have to help her, and in fact doing so wouldn't be easy–it would mean more work and effort on his part. But in response to her questioning, and her persistence–anyone who works with Karen knows she's not giving up easily–he found and gave her the chain of custody notes, a document that describe where evidence goes. That helped Karen figure out where to go and who to call. After an endless maze of mishaps, Karen and Brian literally crawled through a storage facility in East Hartford, looking for a box with the name "Tillman" on it.

My evidence was supposed to be held in a vault managed by the State. Unfortunately, there was a fire at the vault and a lot of the evidence from my era was lost forever. Had my evidence been where it was supposed to be, it would have been destroyed, and I would have no hope of release. Instead, in 1991 the judge who presided over my appeals ordered the evidence sent back to Life Codes through my representatives at Legal Aid. But Life Codes really didn't have a clue what they had. Eventually, after an exhaustive search, a box, the size of a small hat box, was found at Life Codes' storage facility. While nobody had a firm idea where the evidence was, Brian was able to determine from the chain of custody that it had never been compromised, and that it was, in fact, the correct evidence. Another miracle.

They kept the evidence and stored it under lock and key. Without them, my evidence probably would have been lost and I would have had no hope of release. When I think of all the things that had to go my way to get out, to even find the evidence, it's remarkable. Had the evidence been stored at Hartford Hospital where the victim was first taken, it would have been destroyed, because they only keep rape kits for five years (the State has to keep evidence for the term of the sentence). But thankfully, when I lost that appeal, they held my evidence in storage.

Then, in that meeting with Karen and Brian, I heard the words I so longed to hear: we can now do the DNA testing. Karen and Brian were back pushing my case. Hearing that was like having Michael Jordan walk onto a schoolyard playground and ask to be on your basketball team. I was now in the game with the best. I just knew, at that moment, that things were looking up for me.

According to *Scientific Testimony*, an online journal published by Donald E. Riley, Ph.D., of the University of Wisconsin: "DNA is material that governs inheritance of eye color, hair color, stature, bone density and many other human and animal traits. DNA is a long, but narrow string-like object. A one foot long string or strand of DNA is normally packed into a space roughly equal to a cube 1/millionth of an inch on a side. This is possible only because DNA is a very thin string. Our body's cells each contain a complete sample of our DNA. One cell is roughly equal in size to the cube described in the previous paragraph. There are muscle cells, brain cells, liver cells, blood cells, sperm cells and others. Basically, every part of the body is made up of these tiny cells and each contains a sample or complement of DNA identical to that of every other cell within a given person. There are a few exceptions. For example, our red blood cells lack DNA. Blood itself can be typed because of the DNA contained in our white blood cells...A strand of DNA is made up of tiny building-blocks. There are only four, different basic building-blocks. Scientists usually refer to these using four letters, A, T, G, and C...Another term for DNA's building blocks is the term, 'bases.' A, T, G and C are bases...The DNA code, or genetic code as it is called, is passed through the sperm and egg to the offspring. A single sperm cell contains about three billion bases consisting of A, T, G and C that follow each other in a well defined sequence along the strand of DNA...Both coding and non-coding DNA may vary from one individual to another. These DNA variations can be used to identify people or at least distinguish one person from another."

DNA testing could conclusively determine my involvement in this crime. Once they had the evidence secured and located, Karen and Brian spoke with Ed Narus, the prosecutor, to ask for his consent to have a hearing and get the DNA tested. Ed could have made my life more difficult, but I think he has a fair mind and was confident the evidence would determine with certainty the truth. So with his consent, we went before Judge Miano to make our case to conduct DNA testing. On March 22, 2006, I woke up early, as usual, filled with anticipation. I had so much confidence in Karen and Brian that I was able to remain strong despite my being nervous about the outcome. I was shackled, arms and legs, and led to a van. Once at the courthouse, I was prodded like cattle and led to a holding area, and then eventually into Judge Miano's courtroom, where I sat with Karen and Brian. I'm not exactly sure what was said and what was done, because I'm not a legal expert, but I do know this: Karen and Brian were determined and clear and they got what they wanted: the judge's consent to test the evidence. It was like a verbal food fight—nothing like my first trial. They argued, pushing, prodding, objecting, motioning. I was exhausted just watching them, but really pumped up by the action. I went back to prison feeling very confident, knowing I was innocent and that if the test was done correctly, my innocence would finally be proven. But I was still very nervous, so many things had gone wrong for me, and whenever I got my hopes up before they were shattered. So I wouldn't let myself get too excited or feel too good, but I couldn't help but think about getting out. I kept thinking about food, about all the places I could eat, and about all the people I could see. I wondered what life was like outside, and what I would do if I got out. How would I get by? I worried most about the evidence: would they have enough? Could the tests be completed? I'd think about it for a bit, and then tell myself: James, don't do this. Stop worrying. And then I'd try to busy myself in jail by doing push ups, praying and reading the Bible.

In early May, I went to medical, this time with great joy. I was there to have the nurse swab me for the DNA testing. She stuck a long Q-tip into my mouth to capture my saliva. Blood was drawn, and then I was led back down to my cell. I would have given them a kidney at that moment if they asked for it—anything to prove my innocence.

On May 14, 2006, Karen and Brian had a meeting at the forensics lab. Their main concern going into that meeting was whether there would be enough evidence to have a successful test. They told me that there was a spread of crackers and cheese there, but they had no interest in food, just the results. They were relieved when the results came in and were definitive—there was indeed more than enough evidence to test, and not only was there enough genetic material, but they were also able to get consistent results from different sources—underwear, clothes. Whatever result they got would, without a doubt, be definitive.

Karen and Brian were sitting in a sterile and otherwise unremarkable environment when they got the most remarkable news of my life. The lab tech handed them a piece of paper. Five samples showed that I was clear—none of my DNA was present on the evidence. There was still one more test to complete, but Karen and Brian were sure they had enough information to overturn my conviction. Now it was a matter of time, and getting back before the judge. Finally, after 18 years, it felt like the sun was starting to shine.

On June 5, 2006 Karen and Brian came to visit me at Cheshire prison. Sitting together in the Visitor's Center, Karen spoke the words that I'd longed to hear: "James, the DNA testing proves you are innocent." She explained that we were going to go back before the judge and petition him for a new trial, which would eventually lead to my release. However, she would ask the judge to free me until the new trial started. I was confident going into a new trial with this team that I'd be exonerated, but getting out sooner? Wow! The thought of that was mind-blowing. I literally couldn't sit still—not my body, or my mind. I was ecstatic, and they could sense it. "Bring your street clothes, but remember James, you're not out until you're on the other side of those bars," Brian said to me soberly. They may have been hedging their bets, but I knew they would set me free. I had faith in them, in God, and for once, in the process. DNA, it turns out, was literally the key to my release.

I went back to my cell, walked in and looked around. The air conditioning was broken at Cheshire. The air was hot and still, so thick with perspiration you could hang your shirt on it. We were all miserable, and I was determined that this be my last day in prison. I took stock of the place that had held me captive for so long. There wasn't one thing I would miss about prison, and so much I would try to forget.

I gave away everything I had, it was like a prison yard sale. Word quickly spread about the results of my testing. I could almost sense the change in the way people looked at me, from ridicule to reverence; from 'can you believe what he did?' to 'can you believe he was innocent all along?!'

I wasn't sure how things would turn out, but it felt so good to work with Karen and Brian. Their efforts made me feel, for the first time, that someone had my back–that they were going to go into court and give it their all. It was the first time I had any faith in the legal process, and it was driven by my faith in God, that He would show me the way. I was an innocent man, freed once by God, now about to find my physical freedom. Twice in my life I would earn redemption. How lucky I felt sitting there in my cell that warm summer night, a reminder of the power of conviction.

Chapter 27

FREEDOM

On June 6, 2006 I was led out of Cheshire prison. Someone, a guard I think, yelled to me. "Hey James! I saw your picture in the paper. Good luck today. I hope I never see you again!" We drove to the Court, and I just stared out the window, lost in thoughts of my home and my family. What would I do? What will people look like? I started to get nervous about the world outside, and then I told myself, 'first things first–focus on the judge. Don't worry about anything else right now.'

Prior to my hearing, a very violent and destructive person was in the courtroom. I heard bits and pieces of what was going on, and I worried that my case would get delayed for some reason. I begged and pleaded to God that there be order in the court. I didn't want anything standing in the way of my release.

I was taken to the Superior Court in Hartford–the same place where I was sent to jail so many years ago. My feet were shackled and my hands cuffed. I spent 18½ long years in jail, and it was remarkable to me how quickly the Connecticut Innocence Project worked. In a matter of a few months, they were able to consider the facts of my case, find the evidence, test it and get me to this hearing before the judge.

Led into the Court, my hands were un-cuffed when I was seated at a table with Karen and Brian. The first thing I did was thank them for coming. It was enough for me to know they were there to defend me, and I wanted to let them know I appreciated it. They gave hope to a hopeless person, and that is an extraordinary gift. Ed Narus was present on the other side of the courtroom, and Judge Miano presided. The teams were in place, and now it was time to play ball.

Five of the six spots tested showed that my DNA was not present—in other words, that I was innocent. The sixth and final spot, for reasons I don't understand, was not tested as of the morning of my hearing on my petition for release.

The State argued that more time was needed to complete the testing, but there was an admission that the evidence did show that I deserved a new trial. I got the feeling that the judge was on the fence, and that he was considering sending me back to prison. He raised concerns about honoring the legal process, even if I was innocent. Then the sheriff came over to me and whispered, "who do you want to give your street clothes to, since we're going back." I was so upset. I came into this room with evidence proving my innocence, and it still wasn't good enough. I started to feel angry. My legs were shaking; my face tense. My social worker and friend, Katie, was there to support me. She stood in a part of the room where I could see her, and when I made eye contact with her, she was motioning with her hands and saying, "breathe, James, breathe." I paused, took a deep breath and began to calm down. Brian turned to me, looked me square in the eyes and with the utmost confidence said, "James, we're going to get you out." He re-directed his energy and turned back to the judge. Sitting there next to Karen and Brian was like being in a foxhole with five-star generals and having them turn to you in a moment of desperation and say, don't worry, I'll protect you. They unleashed a verbal assault with Brian storming the ridge and Karen taking the flank. It was awesome. Karen objected to the State's request, and in turn demanded my immediate release until a new trial date was set. Brian and Karen spoke so fast I thought they were speaking in tongues. I thought this process might take a long time, but it unfolded pretty quickly. I had no idea what they were talking about, but it was like watching fight at a hockey game—lots of action and stuff flying everywhere. They were citing cases and precedence, working in tandem and leaving no room for anyone to speak. Clearly, Karen and Brian don't like to hear that they can't do something. They were forces of God, and I'm glad they were on my side! Through the power of their argument, with clear reasoning and solid evidence, they hammered the judge. They were relentless. If this was their opening, they weren't going to let it go. It felt so good. Brian argued, "lets just say that piece of evidence comes back inconclusive. Didn't we prove our case here today?" Karen followed, "this is an innocent man. Hasn't he suffered enough? Haven't we proved this man's innocence beyond a reasonable doubt?" The judge nodded in agreement, but Karen kept going. She was on a mission. Finally the judge interrupted, saying "enough, enough," and he agreed to release me pending a new trial, which was set for July 11, 2006—a trial that would eventually be waived by the state.

The judge pounded his gavel, and suddenly, after 18½ years, I was a free man. 18½ years innocent. I was waiting for a climactic moment, something you see on TV or in movies, but it all happened so fast, and as quickly as I was in that court, I was herded out to the holding area, waiting to walk to freedom.

This was the happiest moment of my life. I was filled, overcome, with sheer joy. I sat there alone. This sounds a little embarrassing, but I sat there not thinking about walking out of the doors, but having the freedom to go to McDonalds, Burger King, Dunkin Donuts, Texas Roadhouse or any other restaurant I desired and ordering whatever I wanted from the menu. I was hungry and I had choices and it felt so good.

A warm, sunny summer day, I felt the breeze gently blowing through the open doors just 30 feet away. I was excited, anxious to get out. My mother and a lot of other people were waiting for me. There was a lot of commotion and people walking around. I could feel my heart pounding as the Sherriff walked up to me. I held my feet out to make it easier to un-cuff me, in preparation for finally being released. The sheriff, a middle-aged man with unremarkable characteristics, walked up, stood before me and then paused. He held up his wrist and looked at his watch.

"Looks like it's time to go to lunch," he said. I thought he was joking. I cracked a half smile, studying him.

With that he turned and walked away. I sat there, cuffed, staring at the door that beckoned my freedom. I started to feel angry. He represented everything I hated about prison and law enforcement. My excitement turned to hate, as if I drank a poisoned cocktail, and it started to fill my body. I took a deep breath and I thought about the struggles that Jesus experienced. I told myself: I waited 18½ years for this moment; surely I can wait a little more. I sat there repeating the 23rd Psalm in my mind. "...surely goodness and mercy shall follow me all the days of my life, and I will dwell in the House of the Lord forever."

After he left, another sheriff came over, a woman, and she had a huge smile on her face. She walked up to me, looked me in the eyes and grabbed me by my shirt. I was taken aback, unsure of what was going on. Then she gave me a big kiss on the cheek. "I want to be the first to kiss you when you're free," she said as she sorted through her keys. With an effortless turn of her wrist the cuffs made a shallow clicking sound. And then they opened. I was a free man.

"I'm glad I got to be the one to release you, James," she said as I stood up. I suddenly no longer hated the sheriffs! Somewhat in shock, in a state of disbelief, a little disoriented, I walked towards the doors. I paused a little out of instinct, but nobody tried to stop me. I enthusiastically pushed open the solid steel door, a smile consuming me, overwhelming me, filled with a sense of love and happiness. For that brief moment, everything was blocked out, as if the world around me didn't exist. All I could feel was the warm sun on my body and all I could experience was the vast expanse that surrounded me. I took it all in, intoxicated by the feeling. And then I saw my mother. I ran to her as I had so many times as a child. 18 years ago, I was led away from her, out of her house. It was a long walk back into her arms. We hugged and we cried. There weren't any words that needed to be spoken in that moment. Nothing could appropriately capture the feeling of being free. I could hear people cheering. I was surrounded by a sea of well-wishers and members of the media, but at that moment, all I wanted to do was eat. I was hungry—hungry for food, and hungry for life.

As I walked down the street with my mother I was surprisingly filled with fear. I kept looking around nervously, not wanting to make any mistakes that would get me in trouble. I was constantly looking around to see where the police were. I kept telling myself not to argue with anyone. 'Don't get in trouble, James," I kept telling myself. We went to a Dunkin Donuts. I ordered a coffee and a glazed donut. As much as I craved food, there was one thing, and only one thing, that I wanted do.

I walked on the soft green grass that I spent so many years imagining. I stepped left and right around the obstacles, feeling anxious as I continued searching. I could feel the emotion rising in me. I continued to walk, thinking about him and our life together. I was lost in a world that seemed so foreign to me, so many years ago when we ran free through the streets of Hartford. I stopped and looked down and there it was: my brother's grave and his final resting place. I fell to my knees and prayed to God and Dennis. 18 years of emotion spilled into the fertile ground that held my brother's hallowed remains. As good as my freedom felt, I would give anything to have a moment with him; to say goodbye, to have one last laugh, to have more time with him, brother to brother. "Dennis, I miss you," I whispered to him. "I'm home, little brother. I'm home, and so are you."

Chapter 28

A STRANGE NEW WORLD

I t was great to be out and be free. I loved that I had so many
choices. But getting used to life after prison was like being airlifted
onto another planet. Very few can understand how you have to live
inside, and therefore there aren't many who can help you transition to
life on the outside. On a pure physical level, everything was different.
The city looked different—it was more vibrant and clean, with a lot
of businesses in downtown. TVs were big and flat, and there were so
many channels. I could barely comprehend what the computer could
do—email? You means there's an electronic box that can do so many
things? This is crazy! But I'm pretty with it when it comes to technology,
so I figured it out pretty quickly. When I went to prison, there were
enormous car phones, and most of the phones at home were wired into a
wall. When I got out, there were tiny hand-held cell phones. I remember
that first day out of prison being in a car with my mom and the phone
ringing, and just staring at it. It was so strange to me. That little thing

blew me away! After all, we used phone booths to call home when I was a kid. Cars, one of my passions, had totally changed. They were way more complex and they looked so different. I went to prison at a time when big boxy Cadillacs and Oldsmobiles were all the rage, and now SUVs dominated the landscape. And fashion…don't even get me started. I could have easily spent the next several years just taking in all the changes.

Transition was hard for me. A lot of guys find a way to go back to prison because they can't handle life in the new world. As much as I relished my freedom, I was broke, without a home of my own and unemployed. I walked out of prison with $250 in cash and a form to take to welfare. That's it. 18½ years of my life taken away, and I was literally dropped onto the street. I moved into my mom's house, and I immediately became restless. She was living in a two family house in East Hartford. Gone was my basement palace. Now I was living in an attic with no door and no bathroom. I was grateful for the space, but it wasn't my space, and I struggled with that. Tons of people came over— my story was all over the news. It was great seeing people and catching up, and I felt genuinely happy, but underneath it all, I was nervous. Were they coming back for me? Is this real? Will I have to go back? I spent those early days in a constant state of fear.

I remember so well when a friend of mine who served time with me came over to visit. He was doing well, and he wanted to come by to say hi to me and see how I was doing. We walked outside to look at his new truck, and I was blown away. It was so nice, and I was happy for him. We drove around the block and then he said he had to leave. I reached for the door, and then hesitated, overwhelmed by fear. I simply couldn't open the door. "Hey man, can you drive me home?" I said, somewhat embarrassed. He immediately understood. "Sure," he said, reassuringly, "it goes away over time. It's okay." I was afraid to walk home for fear that something might happen—someone would accuse me of doing something, or somehow I'd get in trouble. I was only a block from my house.

I sat in my bed my first night "home," taking in my new surrounding when the phone rang. I shot out of bed and went into a panic, immediately thinking that someone was on their way to take me, until I realized it was just one of my mom's friends. Instead of feeling elated, as I felt I should have, I went to bed feeling depressed. I knew I was supposed to be happy, but I wasn't. Not yet, at least.

The next morning I went to an office building in downtown Hartford and submitted my welfare form. I received $150 per week. That was a lot of money for me, but not a lot of money by 2006 standards. The story of my release was in the paper, and as a result of that, my attorney, Karen Goodrow, was anonymously contacted by two people. One woman read the story and sent $25. That was such an incredibly kind gesture, and I was grateful for the gift. A second person who read a story in the newspaper sent an anonymous gift that truly made a difference in my life. This singular act of kindness gave me a sense of financial security, and that could have saved my life because it allowed me to focus on my transition to society. This incredibly generous person called Karen and asked for an address, saying he was going to send a check anonymously with one caveat: that nobody know his name. The check was for $10,000. To the person who sent that check: thank you. You made a huge difference in my life, and I am grateful for your generosity.

I wanted to work, but I wasn't sure what I could do, and I didn't know how to start looking. Would I have to tell everyone about being in prison? Would they know I was innocent? Would I have to spend all my time talking about what happened? Could I ever get a normal job? In a lot of ways I was lost and confused. I felt like nobody truly understood me. I didn't have a peer—even guys who were released, they were all convicted. I was the first person in the state released using DNA. There was literally nobody else like me at the time, and that made me feel even more isolated. I knew what I had to do. That week I joined Hopewell Baptist Church in Hartford. I needed to establish my connection to God that I ironically felt more in prison than I did on the outside.

It's hard to believe how many advancements were made in technology during my time in prison. I remember going to the grocery store wanting to use food stamps. I got some food and then stood at the cashier waiting for food stamps. I didn't realize that I had to swipe a card that someone gave me. Things as simple as that were totally foreign to me. When I got out, I didn't understand what ATMs were. You could get cash out of a little box instead of a bank? When I went into prison, you'd go to a bank and cash a check to get money. The idea of sticking a card in a box and getting cash out seemed wild to me. It was nuts. And TVs? They're big and flat now! Where did the big box go? And where did all these channels come from? And what happened to computers? They were everywhere, and they were small. All these things that were a part of life that people took for granted when I got out were foreign to me. And of course, everything was more expensive. Homes, gas, stamps, the price of milk, eggs and bread, the cost of buying a car or going to the movies.

I walked into a local Alphagraphics store and got a part-time job doing copying, which I enjoyed. I was grateful for the work–something to keep me busy. While I was starting to work, my next Guardian Angel was at home reading a newspaper when his daughter asked him a simple yet life-altering question: "Dad, does Mr. Tillman have a job?" The question from his daughter inspired him, and so he called Karen to talk about me. Bruce Douglas, Executive Director of the Capitol Region Education Council (CREC), then called me and invited me in to talk about working for them. To say that Bruce is one of the smartest, most kind and decent people I've ever met in my life doesn't do him justice. Bruce has a generosity of spirit and a clarity of character that sets him apart from most people. CREC is an organization that is bigger than the town board of education but smaller than the State's Department of Education. It was formed in the 1960s as a part of an effort to bring a quality education to as many students as possible, serving 36 towns in the Hartford, Connecticut area. Bruce has a lot on his plate, but he took time to talk to me and help me.

I sat in Bruce's office, nervous, filled with energy, and grateful for the opportunity to talk to someone about work. What I saw in Bruce was not just a kind man trying to help someone who needed a break, but a true visionary, a man who inspires people to do their best, a man who inspires people to be creative and take chances. I sat there in that job interview like I did in my prison cell–watching people, listening to them, and taking measure of them. I watched the way he talked with people. I watched how he carried himself as he walked down the hall to greet me. This is a man I can trust, I told myself. He's a good person. Bruce's career is dedicated to helping young people understand and realize their potential in life, and I was so energized by that. Bruce explained that he had one opening, and that it was a part-time job, but it would provide me with some stability and a regular income, and if nothing else, a place to go to on a regular basis as I worked to become integrated back into life in the year 2006. My job? Fingerprinting! Yeah, I know that sounds crazy, but I got a job fingerprint employees in the educational system for a living. I happily gave up my copy job and started working at CREC.

At the same time, three more Guardian Angels came into my life. John Motley, a former senior executive with Travelers Insurance, is one of the most respected business people in Hartford. He has quite an impressive resume, but to someone who spent as much time as I did in prison, that didn't mean anything to me. What impressed me most was his loving spirit, his generous nature, and his honest, unbiased advice. If Karen had my back during the trial, John had it now that I was out. He quickly earned my trust and respect, and I knew, just knew, that he was with me to help me, not to take advantage of me.

John is like a brother to me. He taught me how to write checks. He took me to buy clothes. He held a fundraiser to raise money to help me buy a car. John helped put my new Dream Team together—a team of advisers that included Tim Fisher and the entire law firm of McCarter & English, who did a lot of work for me and has been extraordinarily helpful since my release. Tim is another one of those rock solid people who was just there for me, and McCarter & English didn't have to help me, but they did because they care and they want to make sure the law works for people like me; Ed Wahlberg of Merril Lynch, who helps me manage my finances and makes sure nobody takes advantage of me; Doug Joseph, my accountant who not only helped with my taxes but also with tax issues involved in my settlement. And finally, I had an incredibly gifted and wise psychiatrist to help with my emotional and psychological transition. I know he doesn't want his name made public, but he was instrumental in helping me work through so many issues. These extraordinary people made sure that I wasn't abandoned once I was released, and that any questions or problems I had—no matter how simple or complex—were handled professionally and in a dignified and respectful manner. They don't treat me like a "client," or condescend to me. They simply represent the best in humanity.

The job gave me structure and stability, John, Tim and the others helped protect me, and I wish I could say that I lived happily ever after, but that wasn't exactly how things turned out for me. Dark days still lay ahead.

Chapter 29

STRUGGLING TO COPE

I had structure in my life, I had good people around me, but I still felt unsettled. There's no way to communicate this without sounding ungrateful, but I was in my 40s and living in my mother's house—I needed to find my own space. Mom was making dinner for me, my older brother was around a lot, and Dennis wasn't there, which made me feel tremendous sadness. A lot of people came by, but only my mother and Dennis visited me in prison, so I began to doubt who was really my friend, and who was just going for the ride. I had trust issues. I also didn't like to be touched—I conditioned myself in prison to react when anyone got close, so I found myself recoiling when people came up to hug me, which I'm sure sent the wrong message. Don't get me wrong, I love to be around people and hug them, but I need to initiate the contact. For a while when I got out of prison, I almost felt under siege. I felt unsettled.

Those feelings would manifest themselves one dark summer night. I was in my room at my Mom's house, feeling really down and empty. I hadn't really settled in at work yet, I didn't feel at home in my mom's house, and I wasn't sure how I fit in. I was given some pills to help me deal with anxiety. I was hanging out in my attic bedroom, lying in bed, just staring at the pills on the table nearby. In that instant, I was overcome with suicidal thoughts. I had won my freedom, but it was a lot harder than I thought it would be. Maybe it was too hard? Dennis should be with me, and he's not. I think, in retrospect, I was mourning his death, and the loss of what could have been some of the best years of my life. Instead of feeling like I had everything, I felt a sense of nothingness. Would I be better off with God and Dennis? I stared at the pills. They lay there, taunting me. I could take them all and just go to sleep, and put this nightmare of a life behind me. I was probably a burden to everyone anyway, and I wasn't sure what, if anything, I had to live for. For the first time since I won my freedom, I contemplated suicide. I reached out to the table and grabbed the pills. I sat up in the bed, clenching them in my hand, reaching out for a bottle of water. As I took a deep breath, tears began to roll down my weathered cheeks. I popped a pill in my hand and chased it with water, putting the rest back on the table, repeating to myself the first words that came into my head, lulling myself to sleep: "Jesus loves you."

Chapter 30

THE COMMUNITY RALLIES

ith some money in the bank, I decided to rent a room from an old girlfriend who lived a few blocks away, on the other side of Main Street. She had a huge house, about 4,000 s.f., so there was plenty of room for me, yet it kept me close to home. I wasn't completely out on my own, but it was a first step. I was worried what my mother would think, but it was something I needed to do. For a while, I flipped back and forth between my new and old spaces. Eventually I would leave both and walk into my own apartment.

After my brush with suicide, I began to turn a corner and my life became more settled and consistent. Hanging out with a friend one day, he caught me off guard with a good question. "Why do you still live in Hartford? If I were you, I would have gotten as far away from here as I could have." I thought about it for a second. It was strange to be in the same place and contributing my money to taxes—the same tax money that was used to wrongfully convict and incarcerate me. Yet I learned my lesson from God and in prison that we should not judge others, so I was reticent to hold a grudge against Hartford or its people. "I live here because I believe in the people of Hartford," I told him. "I want to talk to the kids and give them knowledge and a peek at the choices they can make and how they'll impact their lives. I want to tell them that no matter what they experience, they can endure. I want them to understand that they need to take responsibility for who they are, but that it's never to late to be who you want to be. I want to find the kids that are like me, the ones who are at-risk of throwing it all away, and tell them that God has a plan for them, and a message: he loves you and believes in you." I was a man on a mission. I again started to genuinely appreciate everything, including bills. Walking in to my house one afternoon, I stopped to pick up the mail. I got upstairs and held a non-descript white envelope addressed to me. It was a bill from the phone company. I smiled broadly. It felt so good to get a bill. I can't tell you how much I loved getting bills! I even looked forward to paying taxes. I got a driver's license. John Motley helped me buy a 1989 Mercedes Benz. It had 100,000 miles on it, but despite its age, it was in good shape, and I was so grateful to have my own wheels. I started to feel like I had an identity other than James Tillman, ex-inmate. I felt like a "regular" person for the first time in my life.

It was then, unexpectedly, that the next set of Guardian Angels came in the form of a politician and the lawyer who created the state's Innocence Project: State Rep. Ken Green and Gerry Smyth, esq. Gerry is an extremely talented lawyer with an incredible resume, and Ken is so much more than an elected official—he's a leader. These two men, with the help of many others, led the charge to ensure I received fair compensation for my wrongful conviction. Ken didn't have to act on my behalf. In fact, it may have been politically easier to do nothing, but he recognized an injustice and he wanted to deal with it. I could probably write an entire book about how Ken and Gerry fought to get compensation for me. I'm not a politician, but I do know that getting anything done politically these days takes enormous effort, especially if there is money involved. These people worked so hard, and I know they weren't alone. I don't know all the players involved, but I know there were a lot of key people, like Rep. Doug McCrory, Tim Fisher and Tiffany Stevens and the entire firm of McCarter & English, my accountant Doug Joseph and many members of the State Legislature and their staffs. They put their heart and souls into the work, and I wish I could document everything they did, because they deserve every bit of the attention and spotlight. But the truth is, in some strange way, I needed to keep a distance from this process. This wasn't an esoteric debate about legislation or public policy, this was my life they were talking about. How could anyone put a value on my lost time, on what life meant to me? There isn't a number in the world that could compensate for spending 18½ years in jail, or being called a rapist. There is no price for my integrity. You can't negotiate someone's honor. So the numbers they were talking about—it was a very welcome and I appreciated it very much, but I couldn't allow myself to become too involved in this process. They worked hard and at times it looked bleak, but after enduring everything I did, I kept my perspective, and I kept my focus on my work, serving God and on living my life.

Ken went to bat for me in the legislature, arguing for compensation in lieu of a lawsuit that he figured I would surely file. The state first offered me $250,000, and when Ken told me about that, we had a good laugh. Others who were involved in lawsuits averaged about $1 million for each year in prison. Based on my time served, I could have fought for $18 million. I think part of the reason Ken wanted to do this wasn't just about me, but he knew that others would sadly follow me, and it might be good to have some kind of formula or precedence in place. After the first offer was made, Ken and Gerry went back to get a more fair settlement. Their work kept me out of the uncomfortable position of having to negotiate a settlement, get involved in lengthy lawsuits and most important, of having to re- live 18½ years of hell through another frustrating legal process.

The truth is, I didn't really understand it all—there was just a lot of activity, and I know it was a very difficult thing to pull off. I do know that they put my compensation through as a special act so that it could be exempted from the State income tax. When it was done, Governor Jodi Rell invited me to the annual budget address before the entire legislature. There I stood in the Connecticut's Capitol—the very building in whose shadows I grew up, I was now standing in her legislature as an honored guest. When she announced the compensation for my wrongful conviction, the entire legislature stood and cheered. To me, they are all heroes, and I am grateful to all of them, Republican and Democrat, for working together on my behalf and on behalf of all those who would follow in my footsteps.

Maybe more important than the public recognition in front of the legislature was a private meeting I had with the Governor. At one point near the end of this process, Governor Jodi Rell invited me to her office. She formally apologized to me on behalf of the State of Connecticut, and then she personally apologized to me and my mother. I don't want to describe the details of that conversation because it is something that I need to own, and it is something that I will value for the rest of my life. Her gesture means so much to me, because it showed, more than any amount of money could, that she, as Head of State, valued my life. There weren't two Hartfords for me anymore after that moment—she built a bridge to my Island, and put her arms around it. That meant a great deal to me, and I admire her for her grace and the dignity with which she handled this process. The Governor's apology was a helpful part of my healing process. The state eventually compensated me with $5 million for my wrongful conviction. I know I could have fought for more through the courts, but I wanted to put the whole thing behind me. I needed to move on as fast as I could. A lengthy legal battle would probably mean re-living the hate and the bad experiences that happened in prison, when I desperately wanted to let them go. Some of the guys who got compensated in Boston got $100 million, but they were also very old. I wanted to be able to live my life now with what I had and not have another fight.

Again, I'm certain that a book could have been written about my compensation, the appeal process, the forensic science and some of the other issues involved in the case, but it's one thing to write about my own transformative experiences in prison, and another thing to report about what happened in the Connecticut legislature. I think it's best if those other stories get told by someone else. I can just tell you that as bad as things went earlier in my life, I finally got some breaks, thanks to some really good people.

One of the greatest joys of being out of prison is my freedom to choose—I can go to any restaurant I want, whenever I want. I can wear black, blue or even tan if I want to. I love that I have so many choices.

I find that I look at people differently now that I'm out of prison than I did before I went into prison. I know how it feels to be wrongly accused. I know what it's like to carry the burden of being labeled. So, while I live by God's code now, I hold onto my core value of not judging anyone by labels or appearances. As such, I'm not going to accuse or judge anyone else, including the victim. I want to be known by the choices I make in the context of who I am as a person and how I live my entire life in service to God. I am not perfect and I continue to make mistakes. I should not be looked up to as a role model—I continue to struggle every day to do God's will, and there are times when it is very hard. So if someone was to take a snapshot of me at a specific moment in time, they might be able to label me in a way that isn't true to who I am. I'll take responsibility for it, but it's not fair. That's why I love working so much with teenagers who are in trouble. It's easy to work with super-motivated kids who do well in school and want to volunteer, who maybe have a good home where they're supported. But I find happiness working with those kids who are hard to reach. I continue to go back into prison, or to work with kids who are identified as having potential to go to prison, to try to help them understand that they can make better choices. I want all kids to understand that, despite the labels society, their family, their friends or they put on themselves, that they have a chance to realize and reach their potential in life. I want to help them. This is my life's work. No matter who you are or what you do, rich or poor, teenager or adult, my job is to wake you up out of your sleep and remind you that there is a life worth living if you only release yourself from your own prisons and give yourself fully to God.

The Church has been a constant for me. Your life changes on a dime, and then in the same violent way you're put back into the world and expected to just get going like nothing happened. It has been hard at times to figure out who I can trust, which is why I'm so grateful for my "dream team," but also for my foundation in the Church. It doesn't matter what specific place you go to, but that you are connected to your faith. It grounds me, gives me perspective and fills me with the love and wisdom I need to endure.

Most of all, I want everyone, especially children, to know that if you hold God in your life, you will never be lost. I choose to look at life not for what I lost, but for what I found. I choose to look not at what was taken from me, but that I was given a second chance. I choose to see not that I was a victim, but that I was saved. I choose to believe.

Chapter 31

THE HARDEST TO FORGIVE

Everywhere I go, people ask me about the victim. I have not spoken with her and she has not reached out to me. I don't know why I haven't heard from anyone affiliated with her. I can't answer that. I have to rely on faith that she did the best she could in trying to find the right person. I am very sorry for what she went through—it is an unimaginably horrible crime. I forgive her, and I wish her the best. If I had the opportunity to meet her, I would give her a hug, tell her I forgive her, and say "God Bless You."

If my case does nothing else, it should serve as yet another warning that our public defender's offices are severely understaffed and the attorneys over-worked and under-paid. It should also show the value of the Innocence Project. If you have one dollar to give or any time to spare, please direct it to them.

I knew the guy who committed the crime (I refuse to use his name) because unbelievably I served time with him in prison. On April 13,

2010, he stood before Superior Court Judge David Gold and said three simple words that could have unalterably changed my life so many years ago. "Yes I am." The question? Were you the individual who abducted the victim, restrained her, robbed and sexually assaulted her? Upon my release, one of the questions most frequently asked of me was: "Did they every find the guy who did this?" Now I can finally say, yes, they did. It is my understanding that the DNA used for my exoneration was run through a database, which is how they found the man who did it. I am not sure how he could look at me in prison, knowing I was innocent, letting me serve out his term. Of course I am angry–I have a lot of deep feelings about this, about him, but I cannot let this part of my past go if I hold onto that hate in the present. So as hard as it is for you to believe, as hard as it is for me to do it, I forgive him. I don't condone what he did, obviously, and I think he deserves every bit of punishment he gets. Three words that could have changed my life, "yes I am," and now three words that are all I have in my control to change the course of my life: "I forgive you."

Chapter 32

10 LESSONS LEARNED

Whatcan we learn from my story? What happened to me was unbelievable. How can it resonate with you? Here's my answer: While the details of what I experienced are truly extraordinary, the way I reacted to the events in my life is very ordinary. We all face adversity. We all have problems. We all get lost in prisons of our own making, or are victims of circumstance in life. One need only pick up the paper or talk to a neighbor to understand the little tragedies taking place every day in our lives, with jobs being lost, children turning to drugs, parents suffering from indifference and our society growing more disconnected and polarized. If you learn from my experience and summon the power of conviction in your own life, you can make your own redemption and earn a lasting peace that can sustain you—even carry you through, the rough times.

I didn't write this book to simply offer a laundry list of things for you to do. If I did that, you would read them, maybe do one or two, and go on with your life. Rather, I wanted to bring you through my experiences so that you could internalize the lessons yourself, and feel the power of conviction. So then when you are judged, beaten down, alone, lost or dealing with difficult times, what can you learn from what I went through?

- **People will let you down.** Nobody is perfect. We all have issues, and we all struggle. While we might wish that everyone will always do the right thing, sometimes people are so lost in their own stuff that they can't help, or maybe they just don't want to. I like to believe in the best of people, but I know from my experience that people will let you down, but God never will. So you've got to take care of yourself.

- **Carry yourself with love and respect.** How you carry yourself matters. How you treat people matters. Too many people focus on the end result: what am I going to get from that person? Will I get this conviction? Will I get this deal done? What will I get from that person? What will they do for me? We need to stop asking what, and start asking 'how' more often. How will I deal with that person? The process of a relationship is more important than the end result.

- **Don't judge.** I know what it's like to be judged, to be known as a label, not for who I am. Nobody feels good on the other side of a label, and no life fits comfortably into any box—we're all complex and that's what makes life so interesting. Don't waste it by labeling other people. Judge people based on the content of their character, as Dr. Martin Luther King implored us to do.

- **Stay Strong.** Just because you are willing to forgive people and love doesn't mean that you have to let people walk all over you. Love is tough sometimes. Call people on the bad choices they make, especially when they are hurting others. But strength also comes from admitting when you are wrong, and allowing yourself to be open to love. Strength comes from loving yourself—by how you power your soul, not just pump your body (though staying in good physical shape is also important). One of the things I learned in life is that what some people call "strong" is actually pretty weak.

- **Keep it real.** Commit yourself to being honest and transparent. Anything valuable is rooted in honesty, in being real with someone. It takes a lot of effort to hide from people, but nobody can hide from God. I'm the first to admit that I have faults, that I've made bad mistakes in my life, and if I do something wrong, I own it. Life is short, and we never know when it's going to be taken from us, so better to keep it real.

- **Forgive unconditionally.** You can't just pick and choose who to forgive. For forgiveness to work, you have to forgive everyone, especially those you don't want to forgive. That's why in my case, I had to forgive the accuser and most especially the guy who committed the crime—the same guy who served with me in prison and let me take the fall for what he did. Speak the forgiveness and seek it in person if possible. It was easy for me to forgive some people who weren't directly connected to my incarceration, but the substance of forgiveness really starts with the ones who are hardest to forgive.

- **Let go of the anger and hate.** We're all filled with anger, and sometimes even rage, for things that happen to us in life—even people who seem totally "normal" (as if there is such a thing) carry anger. So whether it's an extreme case like mine, or whether something happened to you at home or work, don't hold onto the anger. If you carry the anger inside you, it will become you, and you need to look no farther than the fights I had in prison to understand that. Or maybe you sometimes find yourself saying something you wouldn't normally say—that's the anger fighting it's way out. When you let the anger go, you allow your real self to come out. You choose to have power over the anger, rather than the anger controlling you.

- **Value what you have.** Life is to short and it changes in a matter of seconds. Learn to love what you have while you have it— treasure all the little things—the hugs, the nice comments, the laughs, the sunrise, the peaceful moments, because you never know when they will be lost.

- **Believe in yourself and never give up.** Conviction can be about what someone does to you, or you can choose to define the word through how you believe in yourself. We really can do anything in life when we believe in ourselves, never give up, work hard and act with honor. If you don't believe in yourself, nobody else will. I know how hard this is, people constantly tell me that they don't know how to get out of the prisons they find themselves in, whether it's addiction, a rough marriage, a bad job, vices or a negative attitude. Clearly, many of us need help—it is hard to go it alone, but at the core, you have to realize that no matter how bad things get, you're alive, you're a child of God, and you are worth loving. Completely broken, alone or abandoned, we each and every day still have to power to control how we approach each moment, each day, and that begins with the will to endure, to just not give up. The hardest step you take in life, without a doubt, is that first lonely step you take towards yourself.

- **Believe in God.** Why are you on this earth? Are we here to just get a bunch of things and then die? Or are we all here connected in some way? And in that connection, in the way that we love ourselves and each other, can we create a force so powerful that we can beat back the tides of hate, scale the walls of indifference, stand up to the oppression, hatred, heartache and negativity? There is every good reason to give up: life is hard. Believe me I know. But when we believe in that loving energy–in God–it can drive us, carry us, and bring remarkable things. I know it because I have seen it. I have lived it. Through the power of conviction, you can change your life and you can unleash your own potential and be who God wants you to be. I believe in you, but more important than that, God believes in you. I was released from my own prison the moment I gave myself to Jesus Christ. Are you going to live selfishly in this world, or are you going to give yourself to something larger than you?

Chapter 33

THE FAITH TO MOVE FORWARD

I was directed to proceed down the long corridor, walls unremarkable in their uniformly drab color. I walked nervously, taking in my new surroundings, making eye contact and taking the measure of my contemporaries. When I finally reached my destination, I walked into the grey windowless room, its menacing concrete block walls constructed to keep me inside. I looked around at my new digs–filled with the basics, but nothing extraordinary. I sat down, finding the newness of the seat awkward, maybe even confining. I listened to the instructions about what I could and couldn't do. It was all so different to me. It was hard to take it all in, and I struggled to do my best. To the outside world, I was supremely confident. Inside, I was a little scared. I began to question myself: Can I do this? Will I be able to make it? As I had so many times, I summoned the power of my conviction. The prison walls were built to confine me. These walls, however, were built to set me free. I sat there, in that room, on a bright sunny September day in 2009, taking my first course at Goodwin College.

One of my heroes in prison was Oprah. Yeah, I know, that's hard to believe–a guy who spent nearly 20 years in prison is a die-hard Oprah fan, but I'd watch her show, or pick up *Jet* Magazine and I was inspired by what she did for kids. Looking at those kids she helped–I saw myself in those kids. What I learned from watching her show, and later from working at CREC, is the critical role education plays in a child's development. She made me realize how important education is to success, and so in prison I started to read more, and told myself that I would go back to school when I got out, in some ways to finish the work I began at Ether Walker. I thought about the old biblical parable: If you give me a fish, I'll eat for a day. If you teach me to fish, I'll eat for a lifetime. My focus at this point in my life is learning as much as I can about fishing!

I have enough money to get by comfortably, but the accumulation of money and things isn't my goal in life. Oprah taught me the value of education, and so if I'm going to talk the talk, I need to walk the walk. What I learn, what I experience, the love I have for life, for learning, for others, that's what sustained me in prison, and that's what's going to carry me through the rest of my life. For me, life isn't about the end result, it's how you live each moment. I'm not sure I'll be able to make it–it's been a long time since I last went to school on a regular basis, but I have faith in myself and in God, and I will go to class every day and do my best to earn my degree.

I got to this point in my life because my love of God enabled me to forgive. If I had carried that hate, I may have never been free, even if I was released from prison. I should not be held up as a role model or glorified in any way. I am not perfect, and I still struggle, to this day, to live as God would have me. Whether you believe Christ is your savior or not, look to my life and my experience as an example of what can happen when you allow yourself to follow God's path, a path of love, forgiveness and community.

Not too long after I was released, I went back to Burges Correctional Institution to give a speech commemorating Black History Month. It was strange to go back into prison, to say the least. When I got there, I saw someone that I worked out with, who was on the boxing team with me. I guess you could say he was a friend of mine. After I was done talking, he stood up in front of a room full of prisoners. He said he believed in his heart that I was a pervert and a rapist. He didn't believe I was innocent, even though he had my back in prison. "You were my friend," he said, "but deep down I didn't believe you. I betrayed you, and I want to apologize." He broke down crying in front of everyone in the room. I told him that I forgave him, and that I was grateful for this opportunity if only to have this chance to seek forgiveness. Had I not gone back into prison that day, had he not had the courage to stand up, this important moment in my life might not have happened. It surely would have been easier for him, in a room full of prisoners, to keep his mouth shut, or to come up to me in private. His public admission was more than just seeking forgiveness, it was about restoring his name and doing something he truly believed was good and right, even in the most adverse conditions. Those words probably cost him—I don't know what happened to him when he went back inside, but I can imagine. But those words also lifted him, in ways he may not even imagine. He made a choice in that moment, a choice to do the right thing, and a choice to take responsibility for what he was thinking. He may be just a scumbag prisoner to you, but on that day, in that moment, he showed true character to me.

We live in a cruel and cynical world, where there is not much to believe in. Clergy, politicians and public officials let us down at times, and family members turn away in indifference and selfishness. So many people live with hate. So many people live life in pursuit of material goods. Rather than read a book to their child, they'll spend time working for that next big deal, or looking for that next thing that will finally make them happy. When that doesn't work, they turn to drugs or alcohol, or they stray from their family. Parents don't talk to children. Brothers don't talk to sisters. And so it goes, from generation to generation. The dysfunction, the cynicism, the negativity, it breeds like a cancer. It is truly the Devil's work.

We live in a world where people find it easier to hate than to love. Where talk radio hosts literally get paid millions of dollars to divide us and call out the worst in others. They seek to disillusion, not inform, and they seek to divide, not engage. The American spirit is weakened, not by others, but by each one of us. We've stopped talking to each other—we mostly yell at each other, and that's sad. It reminds me of what I experienced in prison. Cynicism and hate turns us against ourselves, and each other. Surely these are trying times, many have lost their jobs, and still many more their hope. From Sandy Hook to the Boston Marathon, the American resilience is tested, and people surely question their faith in God. What we don't realize is that God doesn't answer our problems, He gives us the faith to endure, to ultimately choose love over hate, to know that everything can be stripped of us except what we bring to any situation. When we dare to dream, to bring love, then hope endures in every single one of us. We all hold in us the promise of a new day, the chance to fall in love again. I know that sounds like a cliché, but it is and always has been a sustaining truth for me.

It will be so easy for you to put this book down, think it was a nice story, and forget about it, continuing to walk numbly through life. It's so easy to feel overwhelmed with anger about a situation—like how hard it is to find a job or make ends meet, feeling truly hopeless. How, in that moment, can you possibly find love? How, sitting in prison for year after year after year after year, wrongly accused, can I possibly find love? I don't criticize people for feeling hopeless or angry, I honor it. Life is hard, and it certainly is getting harder every day. I'm very real about that. Life has given us every reason to lose hope, to lose our faith. Believe me I understand. But in those moments when your spirit is broken, when you are alone, desperate and feeling like there really is nowhere to turn, nobody who loves you, nobody who believes in you, when you're lost, feeling like you don't know where that next dollar is going to come from or how you're going to find work, when everything is gone, when everything is taken away from us, there is but one last thing to hold onto: faith, a faith born in love. I am inspired by the Holocaust survivor Victor Frankl, who said that everything can be taken from a man except his ability to choose his own way in any given circumstance. It took me a long time to learn that lesson, but I feel its power. And those choices come from a foundation built on faith and trust in God.

You have every right to want to give up at any moment, and there were definitely times when I did. The loss is real and it is painful. There isn't a day that goes by that I don't think of my brother, or my wife's mother, who is going through her own battle with cancer. I don't know much about this life, but I do know one thing: we are not alone. We dedicate this book to those we lost, to those of you who have gone through similar experiences, but most important, we honor them by how we choose to live.

Life is filled with adversity. God presents us with so many choices, some conscious, some unconscious, about how we choose to handle that adversity. Some react selfishly, turning away, or finding it easier to hate, condemn and criticize–blame everyone else for their problems, or blame God. You can have good moments and bad moments, good days and bad days, but that doesn't have to be who you are. You are more than the pain you experience, more than the abandonment you feel, more than the rejection you experience, more than the problems you face; you are also the love you give, to yourself, to others, and ultimately to God. That love won't make your problems go away, but it will make handling those problems more bearable. The problems we face in the world, they will still be very real, very difficult, but we can face them through the triumph of our collective spirit. I spent 18 years in prison, but what ultimately released me was an unyielding belief in myself and a choice to dedicate my life to God, to His love, not to perfection in me, but towards the perfection that is God's love for us. That's not a God that kills people in the name of religion, hurts others or seeks to divide us along political lines, but an ever loving God that sustains us when all else is gone, whether you're confined to a physical prison as I was, or another kind of psychological prison. This book explains the choices that I made, poor ones fueled by my hurt and anger, and inspired choices realized through a transformational forgiveness and the power of my conviction.

But as you think about your own life and reflect on what I experienced, I close this book with a question for you: When faced with your own challenges in life, what will you choose?

ABOUT THE AUTHORS

James Tillman, one of the most positive and inspirational people you will ever meet, spent over 18 years in prison for a crime he did not commit, and was the first person in Connecticut released through the use of DNA. Remarkably, James calls his experience in prison, "a gift," because it ultimately changed his life for the better, helping him learn that everything can be taken except our ability to choose what we believe. James, who never had the opportunity to go to college, is now pursuing a degree in social work at Goodwin College in Hartford, CT.

Jeff Kimball, co-writer, is the author of "Community, Connection & Conversation: Making Social Media work for Business." Jeff's varied career began in Washington, D.C. as a press aide to U.S. Sen. Joseph R. Biden, Jr. and a press and political aide to U.S. Sen John D. Rockefeller IV. Jeff, a heralded screenwriter, also worked as a PR executive on Wall Street and as marketing and media consultant to start-ups and non-profits. Jeff, who lost his wife and parents to cancer, is now the Executive Director of Circle of Care, an organization that supports children with cancer and their families.

CPSIA information can be obtained
at www.ICGtesting.com
Printed in the USA
FFOW03n1557130315
11736FF